COACHING
for the
Love of the Game

Jennifer L. Etnier, Ph.D.

COACHING
for the
Love of the Game

A Practical Guide for
Working with Young Athletes

THE UNIVERSITY OF NORTH CAROLINA PRESS

Chapel Hill

Cover illustration: © iStockphoto.com/kali9
Sports icons in figs. 3.2 and 3.3 © iStockphoto.com/leremy and Malachy120;
basket illustration in fig. 5.2 © iStockphoto.com/studiogstock

All figures and tables were created by the author unless otherwise noted.

Designed by Jamison Cockerham
Set in Scala, Strangeways, Bunday Slab, and College
by Rebecca Evans

Manufactured in the United States of America

The University of North Carolina Press has been a member
of the Green Press Initiative since 2003.

LIBRARY OF CONGRESS CATALOGING-IN-PUBLICATION DATA
Names: Etnier, Jennifer L., author.
Title: Coaching for the love of the game : a practical guide
for working with young athletes / Jennifer L. Etnier.
Description: Chapel Hill : The University of
North Carolina Press, 2020. | Includes index.
Identifiers: LCCN 2019032092 | ISBN 9781469654829 (cloth) |
ISBN 9781469654836 (paperback) | ISBN 9781469654843 (ebook)
Subjects: LCSH: Coaches (Athletics)—United States. |
Exercise for youth—United States. | Leadership.
Classification: LCC GV711 .E86 2020 | DDC 796.07/7—dc23
LC record available at https://lccn.loc.gov/2019032092

To the millions of youth athletes playing for the love of the game, and to the coaches, administrators, and officials who are dedicated to fostering that love.

CONTENTS

COACHING

for the
Love of the Game

The Why of This Book

So, you have this book on coaching in hand, and now you might be wondering why anyone would write such a book and why you need to read it. Let me start with the second "why" first. Why do you need to read this book? Because you are a youth sports coach. As a youth sports coach, you have the opportunity to impact children in ways that will stay with them for the rest of their lives. And you have the chance right now to make sure that those impacts are positive rather than negative. What kind of a coach do you want to be? If you want to be a great coach, then it's not about your win/loss record. To be a great coach, your goals must extend well past the field, gym, court, or pool. Being a great coach goes way beyond drills, scrimmages, and play calls—that's the easy stuff. Being a great coach requires that you meet the athletes where they are, that you treat them as the special and unique individuals that they are, and that you put their development as people above all else when you are working with them. You need this book to give you the tools to have a positive, long-lasting effect on your athletes. Your young athletes are incredibly special. They are developing rapidly in terms of their physical abilities, their cognitive skills, and their social acumen. And your athletes' parents have entrusted you, as their coach, to nurture them and to foster their development within the trappings of your sport. When the athletes come to you, they will be excited to learn and to have fun. But they will also be looking to you as one of the adults in their world who can teach them to navigate the many changes they are experiencing as they grow toward adulthood. They are looking for more than the X's and O's of the sport. They are looking for role modeling, fair treatment, a positive attitude, and unwavering support. They will call you "Coach,"

and that title carries with it both enormous responsibility and unlimited opportunity. As Spider-Man's uncle Ben says, "With great power comes great responsibility." This quote epitomizes what it means to be a coach. You've taken on the mantle of being a youth sports coach—so it is critical that you wield your powerful influence responsibly. This book will help you live up to the title of "Coach" by ensuring that your athletes have a positive sports experience, develop as individuals, and grow to love the game.

....

KEY QUOTE *The Power of a Youth Sports Coach*

With great power comes great responsibility.

SPIDER-MAN'S UNCLE BEN

....

I have written this book to serve as your go-to resource for the most critical aspects of your role as a coach. This book is written for you if you are a first-time volunteer coach, but it is also written for you if you are a paid coach who has been involved in youth sports for years. It is written for recreational coaches, competitive coaches, and elite coaches. It is also written for officials and league administrators. If you are working with youth athletes in any setting, this book is written specifically for you, and it is designed to help you move beyond the ephemeral goals of sports success to the permanent goals of life success.

Let me also explain why I wrote this book. With three children, my family is currently knee-deep in youth sports. This has brought great joy to my partner and me as we have watched our children accomplish personal goals, develop their sports skills, enjoy competition with their friends, and take on increasing leadership roles with their teams. But on the flip side, I cannot tell you how many times I have woken up at 4 a.m. worried about the negative impact that a coach's behavior might have on a young child. Most of the time, this sleep-ending fear hasn't even been for my own child. It's been for someone else's son or daughter whom I've seen mistreated, ignored, insulted, or demoralized by his or her coach. I lie there in the wee hours of the morning trying to figure out how to approach the coach to tactfully explain how his or her behavior is having a negative impact on the child. I have spoken to coaches in person, I have written letters, and I have sent emails, and sometimes these communications have made a difference. But one morning I woke up and realized that addressing one coach at a time is not good enough, not fast enough, and not effective enough, given the breadth of the problem. I felt like I was putting buckets under the holes in a leaky roof! By writing this book, I hope to contribute to building a new roof. My goal is to reach large numbers of coaches and other adults involved in youth sports and share knowledge regarding how to best work with youth athletes in the hopes of having a positive impact on kids across the country.

Youth Sports Today

Have you noticed that youth sports today are different from decades ago? If you head out to a park or a field near your home, you are unlikely to see a group of children playing sports in an informal way. There is probably no pickup basketball, Wiffle ball, capture the flag, kick-the-can, or hide-and-seek being played near you. If children are outside and active, you will notice right away that they are typically involved in organized sports under the guidance of their adult coaches and with their parents, family, and friends as spectators.

Clearly, sports have changed dramatically from an activity that children used to enjoy in free play settings to a formal, structured, organized activity that cannot operate without adult involvement. In fact, youth sports have come to be viewed as an early training ground for elite-level athletes, and coaches at all levels have fallen into the trap of thinking that winning is what matters in youth sports. You may think I'm crazy, but the honest truth is that winning doesn't matter one bit in youth sports. There, I said it out loud, and I would scream it from the mountaintops. WINNING DOESN'T MATTER IN YOUTH SPORTS! What matters is that the athletes have positive experiences, improve their skills, have fun, learn to work hard, and develop as individuals. And the counterintuitive point here is that if athletes do all of these things, the chances of winning increase. So, it's not the "winning" per se that matters. Winning matters only to the extent that we let it matter to the athletes. It is our interpretation of winning that influences how our athletes learn to deal with both winning and losing. As a youth sports coach, you play a pivotal role in terms of affecting the experiences of your athletes, and that is why you need this book.

Throughout my own sports experiences, I have certainly seen the wide range of skill sets, personalities, and styles that coaches bring to their sport. I have played for, worked with, and observed coaches who run the gamut from wonderful to horrible in terms of the impact on their athletes. Much of the time, the coach's impact is positive resulting in a powerful, constructive influence on the athletes. But for many athletes, unfortunately, the impact is quite negative. For example, I have witnessed young athletes who have started a season excited to play and have quit before the season ends because the practices are not fun and they get minimal opportunities to play. I have seen young athletes who initially desire to play at a high level but then burn out and leave their sports forever because of the extreme pressure and high commitment expected from an early age. I have also seen coaches appear to lose their minds as they focus so much on winning that they scream at their athletes, officials, and even athletes on the other team. These types of negative behaviors occur all too often, and you have probably seen examples in your own experiences.

Let me share some personal experiences that further illustrate these points. As my children have entered the youth sports world, I have felt the need to be an advocate for them, to be a well-informed consumer, and to be a sleuth in finding out all that I can about coaches and sports organizations before allowing them to play. I have heard my children say things like, "Can we quit playing for this team and just play at home?" and "I want to switch from soccer to cross-country because cross-country is fun." These comments drive me crazy. In both cases, the statements were in response to the behaviors of the coaches. How can coaches allow athletes on their team to feel like this? It happens all too often and surely cannot be purposeful on the part of the coaches. Rather, I imagine that it is happening because *we do not do a good job of providing coaching education for the large numbers of coaches who are interacting with youth athletes.* Most youth sports coaches have not received any formal education on coaching and so are left to fend for themselves in terms of interacting with the athletes. In fact, there are no centralized requirements for coaching education at any level in the United States. As a result, we often see negative behaviors repeated as coaches treat their athletes in the way that they were treated, in ways they have seen glamorized in the media, or in ways that are driven by motives of winning rather than in ways that focus on development.

Recently, I taught a graduate-level class focused on youth sports. My interactions with the students in that class reinforced my belief that something has to be done to improve the experiences of youth athletes. The students in the class were studying to be practitioners in youth sports or other levels of sports. Hence, they were all people like me who see value in sports and the positive experiences sports have to offer to young people and adults. But the stories these students told of their own personal experiences with sports were remarkable in their negativity. The most memorable story was about a high school soccer team, and it wasn't the actions of the coach that were important here but rather the lack of action. Games were played at a location that allowed for cars to be parked in a lot directly behind the goals. One of the parents would sit in the car rather than watch from the bleachers. Any time that his son made a mistake, the father would lay on his horn until his son would look his way and acknowledge that he had heard. Imagine this if you will. Here you are, a sixteen-year-old trying your hardest in a game only to be publicly attacked by your parent in a way that is demeaning and inappropriate. And in this situation, the coach, officials, and administrators did nothing to intervene. Events like this make me realize how critical it is to educate our youth sports coaches and to get our coaches on board in terms of creating a climate in sports that makes playing a positive experience.

So, I have written this book for you, and my goal is to provide ideas, suggestions, evidence, and guidance that will help you have a positive impact. There are two related points that I would like to share before we dive in. First, I have written this book because of my unwavering belief in the value of youth sports and my confidence that youth coaches want to have a positive impact on their athletes. My belief in the value of youth sports comes from my personal love for physical activity and sport, my long history of involvement in both, and my knowledge that a positive youth sports experience is critical for our children. Second, I am confident that coaches who enter the world of youth sports desire to be the best they can be in terms of working with their athletes. I trust that most coaches have goals that are consistent with the goals of their young athletes and are motivated to be a positive influence on the athletes entrusted to them. Allow me to expand upon each of these reasons.

Love, History, and Value

I love physical activity and sports! As a former athlete, a parent of youth athletes, a sports psychologist, and a former coach, I have had a lot of experience participating in sports and interacting with others who are currently engaged in sports. My involvement in sports started at a young age. I fondly remember my dad hitting softballs to me in the front yard when I was six years old. I have warm memories of my mom teaching me to play tennis in elementary school and our joy in playing together in mother-daughter doubles tournaments when I was a teenager. Throughout my childhood, I played as many sports as I possibly could. I lettered in softball, basketball, and soccer in high school. I played volleyball and tennis for fun and was on the swim team in the summer. I learned to water ski, sail, windsurf, and snow ski when the weather and opportunity allowed. In fact, anytime I could, I was outside playing. As a result of my constant sports participation, I developed as a multisport athlete who loved to play just for the fun of playing.

When I was in college, I continued to play multiple sports, but I focused on soccer. I had the opportunity to play in college and was selected for state-level select teams and to play semiprofessionally. I have been coaching soccer since I was thirteen years old, have obtained national coaching licenses from the United States Soccer Federation, and have coached from the U7 level (under seven years old) to the collegiate level. I have written a book called *Bring Your "A" Game*, which is designed to present sports psychology skills such as goal setting, emotional management, and mental imagery to young athletes. I regularly provide educational presentations to parents, coaches, and athletes. As a parent, I exposed my own children to sports and physical activity in informal ways when they were young and ultimately started enrolling them in organized youth sports when they were in elementary school. Now, I enjoy watching them run track and cross-country and play tennis, soccer, volleyball, and basketball as middle schoolers.

As an adult, I have chosen to focus on sports and physical activity for my career. As a kinesiology professor, I have the opportunity to conduct research and teach about the benefits of human movement. We have a strong body of evidence that physical activity has both physical and mental health benefits that are associated with more positive lifestyle behaviors, greater success, and better overall health (see fig. I.1). We know that children who are active experience benefits that are apparent during their school-age years and into adulthood. We also know that people who are active when they are young tend to be more active as adults and even as older adults. Because youth sports can provide children with confidence, experiences, and skill sets that promote their

ACTIVE KIDS DO BETTER IN LIFE
WHAT THE RESEARCH SHOWS ON THE COMPOUNDING BENEFITS

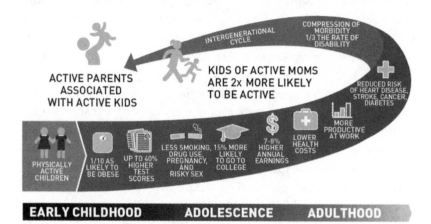

Figure I.1. Physical activity in childhood is associated with a variety of positive outcomes, including better health, more positive behavioral choices, better academic performance, and higher earnings. Figure adapted with permission from the Aspen Institute, Project Play, http://youthreport.projectplay.us/the-solution.

ability to be physically active as adults, we should do everything we can to make sure that the youth sports experience is positive for every child.

In sum, I am a physical activity enthusiast, a lover of sport, and an advocate for sports and physical activity participation by all because of the inherent joy of being physically active and the long-term benefits of maintaining a lifetime of physical activity. And, because you will be coaching young athletes in sport, you have the opportunity to help ensure that they stay on this path of loving sports and being physically active for a lifetime.

Coaches Want to Have a Positive Impact

I have also written this book because *I know that you want to make a positive impact on your athletes.* In my opinion, the rapid growth of youth sports organizations in the absence of any state- or national-level oversight has resulted in coaches coming into sports with good intentions but being left to fend for themselves in terms of understanding how to be a good coach. If coaching were easy, everybody could do it well.

But it's not easy, and some education is required to learn how to be a good coach. Since you are taking the time to read this book, clearly you are committed to being the best coach that you can be. I'm not talking about being the best coach in terms of the X's and O's of tactics and techniques but about being the best coach in terms of the X's and O's of relationships, role modeling, and the development of confident, happy, and motivated young people. You are undoubtedly giving your time and energy to coaching youth athletes for the right reasons. That is, you come into the role of coach with aspirations of having a positive impact on the athletes who have been entrusted to you. As such, this book is designed to provide you with guidance, support, explanations, and rationale for how to ensure that you have the intended effect on your athletes and how to help them get the most out of their sports experience.

The purpose of this book is to share ideas related to excellence in coaching, when excellence is defined as making the youth sports experience as positive as possible. My goal is to help you learn to interact with your players in ways that will help them love their sport, advance relative to their potential as young athletes, and maintain an interest in physically active behaviors. My hope is that this book will contribute to the growing efforts to pull youth sports back from the brink of professionalism. By offering explanations, advice, examples, and guidance, I intend to help you make sports a more positive experience for the youth athletes under your care. As coach, you have the opportunity to make sports a great experience for your athletes, and my goal is to provide you with the tools to do this.

....

CHAPTER ONE

Why Participate in Youth Sports?

....

Before we dive into specific topics, it is important to understand some of the basic reasons that participants become involved in youth sports. Two of the primary groups involved in youth sports are obviously the coaches and the athletes. So, let's start by considering two questions that relate to their participation: Why are you coaching? And why are the children playing? Once we've taken a broad look at the answers to these questions, we will have a foundation from which to move forward in terms of learning how to achieve your goals as a youth sports coach. After that, we'll consider the reasons children choose to drop out of sports and how those also relate to your role as a coach.

Why Are You Coaching?

For fifteen years I worked with the United States Soccer Federation, contributing to their coach education program. One of the first questions I asked the coaches attending these national coaching schools as a way to get them to self-reflect was, "Why are you coaching?" This question provided invaluable insight into their motivations for coaching in the first place and what their goals were as coaches. So, ask yourself that question right now. Why are you coaching? Why did you say *YES* when asked to coach or, more remarkably, why did you volunteer to coach a youth sports team? Maybe you are excited about your upcoming opportunity to coach, or maybe you had your arm twisted and are reluctantly entering this job. Either way, you've said yes, and so it's important to now think about what this commitment means and why you ultimately agreed to do it.

Deciding to coach a youth sports team might have been a hard decision for you. The commitment to being a youth sports coach is not trivial. You will be giving up one or more nights a week to lead practices; you will be responsible for the players at practices, games, and tournaments; and you may have commitments that extend beyond the sport itself, such as washing team uniforms, mowing the field, or organizing after-game snacks and arranging car pools. You will be interacting with parents, officials, other coaches, and administrators on topics that include playing time, league rules, player expectations, and schedule changes. You may be coaching a team that loses every game or a team that wins a lot and travels to numerous away events. You will be sacrificing family time and free time to prepare for practices, to attend practices, and to coach at every game, event, or meet. What is amazing is that, unless you are a full-time coach, you are probably doing all of this on top of a full-time job, and you will not be paid much or at all for your time and efforts. So, given all of these facts, the reasons you said yes must be compelling.

Take a minute to think about your reasons for coaching and answer this question: Why are you coaching? (Use the space below for your response.)

_____

_____

_____

When I have asked this question of coaches in the past, the answers have been varied and include the following:

- Because my child is playing, and I want to spend more time with him/her.
- Because my child is playing, and no one else would do it.
- Because I know a lot about the sport and want to share my knowledge.
- Because I enjoy working with kids.
- Because I played this game as a child and had a great experience.

- Because I want to give back to a game that gave so much to me.
- Because I love this game and want to share my enthusiasm with kids.
- Because I think sports help kids develop character.

....

KEY POINT *Coaching for the Love of the Game*

Coaching for the love of the kids and the love of the game means that

- having fun should be a primary focus,
- practices should be developmental,
- playing time should be shared and close to equal,
- feedback should be constructive, and
- the development of your athletes should supersede competitive outcomes.

....

Do any of these match what you wrote down? Given that the reasons listed above are prominent motives for coaching, it is likely that at least one of these describes a reason you have chosen to coach. So, let's look at them more closely. If we accept that the first two listed are essentially the same as saying "Because my child is playing, and I love my child," then you will notice that all of these reasons are focused on extremely positive emotions and desirable benefits for children. They focus on the love of the game, the positive affective experiences of playing, and the opportunities for growth and development by young athletes. Perhaps we could aggregate these reasons into one main theme: "for the love of the kids and the love of the game." This is definitely a compelling reason to coach and is an important mantra for coaches to keep in mind as they work with their athletes. If this mantra describes your reason for coaching, then it should guide every decision that you make with your athletes. *In other words, if you are coaching because you want to infuse a love of the game into the youth athletes you are working with, then your practices, feedback, lineups, playing-time decisions, interactions with parents, and pregame, halftime, and postgame talks should all reflect that goal.* Everything you do should be consistent with making sure that the kids look forward to practices with eagerness, that they can't wait for the games, and that they end the season wanting to play even more than they did the day they joined your team. Every decision you make should reflect your goal of ensuring that the athletes have fun and maintain or increase their interest in the sport.

....

SCIENTIFIC EVIDENCE *Why They Play*

When synthesized across sports and ages (Weiss and Williams 2004), the most consistent reasons that children give for their participation in organized sports include these:

- They enjoy sports experiences.
- They like making friends and strengthening friendships.
- They have a desire to improve or demonstrate physical capabilities.

....

Why Are They Playing?

Now that we've thought about why you are coaching, let's consider the athletes. Why do you think they are playing? If you ask five- and six-year-olds why they are playing, you might be surprised by their answer. Many of them may tell you that they are playing because their parent signed them up and dropped them off! And that may be the primary reason a child is on your team if you are coaching young children. Once children are in later elementary school and middle school, they tend to voice their opinions more strongly and so have likely self-selected their sports choices.

So, let's think about what the kids tell us. They say that they are playing because of the enjoyment and fun of playing, for positive social reasons, and because they want to get better and have a chance to show their skills. Do you see the consistency with what the coaches said? The coaches said they were coaching for the love of the game, because of the positive affective experiences of playing, and to contribute to the growth and development of young athletes. Given that coaches and kids are expressing essentially the same reasons for being a part of the sport, then one might expect sports to always be a positive experience in which coaches foster enjoyment and love of the game in their athletes, and athletes respond by having fun and enjoying every moment of their time in this sport. But, unfortunately, we know that this is often not true. If you've read the book *Why Johnny Hates Sports* (Engh 2002), which was written by a youth sports advocate, you can get a glimpse into some of the reasons this love affair with the game doesn't always come to fruition.

Why Do They Quit Playing?

So now let's take a look at why children might choose to stop playing a sport. We know that a large percentage of children drop out of organized youth sports each year (Eitzen and Sage 2009). Although some of these children are simply switching to school teams, trying other sports, or choosing leisure activities (for example, cycling or hiking), we also know that many drop out of organized sports completely by the time they are thirteen years old and do not pick up other forms of physical activity (Eitzen and Sage 2009). Clearly, this has implications for their physical health during their school years, but this also has implications for their physical activity levels as adults as many of them begin a trend to being more sedentary. So, when children drop out of a sport, what are their reasons? What do you think the *top* reason is?

_____

_____

_____

That the sport is no longer fun is the number one reason identified by almost 40 percent of youth athletes for having dropped out of a sport. This is shocking, isn't it? How can it not be fun? It's a game! The whole point of the game is to have fun, and the number one reason children started playing sports was because it was fun! If children are not having fun in sports, then there must be something going drastically wrong that is contributing to a dramatic alteration of their perceptions.

So, what happens in sports that makes kids decide that the game is not fun? Before answering that question, we must first consider how "having fun" is defined by youth athletes. In youth sports, fun can be had in many different ways that run the gamut from doing a cool team cheer to getting playing time. Scientists report that the top sources of fun in youth sports come from being a good sport, trying hard, and being exposed to positive coaching (Visek et al. 2015). Being a good sport is further defined by youth athletes as playing well as a team and as giving support to and receiving it from teammates. Trying hard is characterized as giving your best, working hard, being active, playing well, being strong and confident, and competing. Positive coaching is the third contributor to having fun in sports, but in many ways it supersedes the other two contributors because the coach has such a powerful impact on the entirety of the athletes' sports experience.

....

KEY POINT *Positive Coaching*

A positive coach

- creates a climate focused on learning and improvement,
- treats the athletes with respect,
- develops relationships,
- shows compassion and empathy,
- is encouraging,
- is a good role model,
- communicates clearly and consistently,
- is knowledgeable, and
- is understanding of mistakes.

....

According to youth athletes, positive coaching is defined by how a coach treats his or her athletes. Although you may not be able to dramatically increase your knowledge of the game in a short period of time (the X's and O's of techniques and tactics), you will notice that all the other aspects of positive coaching reflect the X's and O's of relationships, compassion, and being a good role model and therefore are completely under your control. That is, you can control your behavior at games and practices to be a good role model, you can communicate clearly with athletes to create solid relationships, and you can respond positively to mistakes to demonstrate your compassion and empathy for your athletes. Right this minute, you can make the commitment to use positive coaching techniques (those that focus on how you treat your athletes) to ensure that your athletes have fun playing their sport with you as the coach. Take a minute to pledge that you will be a positive coach. By making this commitment and sticking to it, you increase the chances of your athletes persisting in your sport and developing a love for the game.

COMMITMENT STATEMENT

I, _____ ,

have made the commitment to be a positive coach. As a part of this commitment, my primary goal is to ensure that the children on my team have fun and develop their interest and love for the sport. I will do everything in my power to achieve this goal by using positive coaching techniques in practices, in games, and in all interactions with my athletes, their parents, other athletes and coaches, and officials.

SIGNATURE   DATE
_____

The Elephant in the Room— What about Winning?

Obviously if we are talking about sports, then we must acknowledge that sports have outcomes, and these outcomes determine winners and losers. So, you might be wondering how winning figures into the youth sports experience. As I mentioned in the introduction, winning matters only to the extent that we allow it to matter. And, in youth sports, the truth is that *winning isn't important at all!* In fact, winning is *not* an outcome that is identified as important by most youth sports coaches and athletes.

Many youth coaches recognize that winning is not in their control, and this is a critical first step to letting go of winning as your ultimate goal. Winning is not in your control for a variety of reasons. For one thing, you are the coach, not the athlete. You can teach your athletes all that you know, you can help them develop to reach their potential, and you can motivate them and teach them strategy. But you cannot play for them. Hence, winning is never in your control. Another reason winning is out of your control is because youth sports typically do not provide a level playing field. When youth teams are created, the players are often added to teams based upon where they live or the nights of the week they are available to practice. As a result, teams are often dramatically uneven in terms of skill level. Furthermore, at a very young age, it really only takes a handful of physically strong, skillful kids to allow one team to dominate over the others. You can see it in the score lines where soccer scores are 6–0, football games have scores of 63–6, and baseball and softball leagues enact a "mercy rule" when teams get ahead by ten runs. This disparity is in distinct contrast to collegiate and professional sports. In collegiate sports, there is typically great uniformity across conferences because these conferences have the same resources available to put into the recruitment of their athletes. In professional sports, the draft system and salary caps are designed specifically to help maintain competitive parity. These variables that help ensure an even playing field at higher levels of competition do not exist in youth sports. In fact, depending upon the league, the opposite may be true, where strong teams are allowed to stick together and new teams form from players with unknown ability levels. As a result of having uneven teams to begin with, many youth coaches appropriately realize that winning and losing is partially predetermined. Therefore, the only things coaches can control are how they approach the development of their team to increase its likelihood of success and how they help players cope with outcomes.

· ·

KEY POINT *Winning*

Winning is a secondary outcome to the skillful execution of the sport with high levels of intensity, investment, and passion. When coaches and athletes focus on winning at the expense of the process required to be successful, they will ultimately fail. When coaches and athletes focus on the process required to be successful, winning becomes possible.

· ·

So, what do athletes think about winning? Athletes of course care about winning. They keep track of their season record and may be aware of the score in games even in leagues where the score is not officially recorded. They may recognize that winning can be an indicator of their ability, but many also acknowledge when they are outmatched and can accept defeat when the outcome is not under their control. When athletes do mention that they care about winning, they typically add the caveat that winning is valuable only when they play against an equally skilled team. The athletes therefore clearly recognize that winning is important only when there is a level playing field and understand that the sense of accomplishment comes when they try hard and improve. The key here is that as coach, you must display this same interpretation of winning as an outcome that is important and achievable only when it reflects a focus on having fun, improving, and trying hard. The slogan "Winning isn't everything, it's the only thing" is often attributed to Vince Lombardi, much to his chagrin (Lombardi 2001, 230), but was actually first said by football coach Red Sanders (Lombardi 2001, 226; Lombardi 2003, 51). This slogan may be appropriate in professional sports where the competition level is even, where controllable factors can determine the outcome of the event, where sports are obviously a business, and where winning is the sole determinant of success. But it is completely inappropriate for youth sports. However, there is another similar quote that is attributable to Vince Lombardi: "Winning is not everything, trying to win is everything" (Lombardi 2001, 229). This is clearly a more suitable mantra for youth sports because the focus at that level should be on effort. In youth sports, winning is often out of the control of the athletes and the coach and, importantly, is secondary to the intrinsic motivators of having fun, trying hard, improving, and demonstrating physical ability.

Why This Matters

There is great consistency in the reasons children play sports and the reasons adults coach youth sports. It's all about the love of the game, which includes a love for the sports experience itself, a desire to demonstrate ability, and the rewards of being a part of a supportive group. As coach, you are largely responsible for your athletes' experiences—it is your duty to do everything you can to ensure that they have positive ones. You will know you are doing well if the children are excited to come to practice, are engaged in your activities, and look forward to competitions. You will know you are doing well if their enthusiasm for the game increases during their time with you. You will know you are doing great if the players come back to your team again for a second season. I am confident that you are coaching because you want to have a positive impact on your athletes, and you are reading this book because

As the coach, your young athletes will look up to you literally and figuratively. They are looking to you to motivate them, to teach them, to model appropriate behavior, and to increase their love of the game.
Illustration by Dominy Alderman.

you want the skill set to help you reach that goal. So, I compliment you on your beginning efforts to be a great coach. A great coach is one who ensures that every child (regardless of skill level or ability) under your tutelage feels valued, respected, cared for, and encouraged. If you can make your athletes feel this way, you can be a great coach and help your athletes develop a love for the game.

Activity

Think back to your time as a youth athlete. Reflect on the following questions and consider how your answers relate to your own behavior as a coach.

1. You are coaching in part because you love the game. What is it about the game that you love?
2. You are coaching in part because you care about kids and you care about your child. What do you want them to get out of their time playing with you?
3. What benefits did you receive from your participation in youth sports? How can you help ensure that your athletes experience these benefits?

4. What do you remember as being important about the good coaches whom you had when you were young? Why were they "good"?
5. What were your parents like during your participation? How did their behavior influence your sports experience?
6. Were there any negatives to your sports experience? If so, consider how you might use your role as coach to minimize these negatives for the athletes you are working with.

CHAPTER TWO

Youth Sports Today

In the introduction, I mentioned that youth sports have changed in recent decades. Today, youth sports look and function increasingly like professional sports. Let's think about professional sports first. Professional sports use a business model in which teams that are successful capture larger shares of the available revenues. For this reason, professional coaches must interact with their athletes in ways designed to increase the likelihood of winning games and championships. And professional athletes must treat their sports participation as a job—a place where they work and where their value is judged by their performance. Now let's consider youth sports. Youth sports became an institution in response to decreasing opportunities for children to engage in free play in their communities. As families moved to suburbs and cities became less safe, youth sports organizations stepped in to provide safe environments for children to participate in sports activities. Initially, youth sports were designed to engage children in sports for intrinsic reasons related to enjoyment, competition, physical activity, health, and character development. However, the structure of youth sports today suggests that the goals have changed. In fact, it is important to remember that youth sports today exist as a business.

The Business of Youth Sports

Although most youth organizations operate as nonprofits for tax purposes, that doesn't mean that coaches and administrators within the organizations can't do well financially! The nonprofit designation simply means that any profits generated by the organization must be put back into the organization. Decisions are made by a governing board with respect to the use of those profits, which can include raises for coaches and administrators. Given this scenario, there is clearly a motivation for those in charge of the sports organizations to increase the organization's profits. Altogether, youth sports organizations in the United States that operate as nonprofits spend over $5 billion annually (*Columbus Dispatch* 2010). And there are increasing numbers of youth sports organizations that are beginning to operate as for-profit entities, which allows profits to be distributed among the owners of the organization. In total, considering both for-profit and not-for-profit organizations, one estimate suggests that as much as $15.5 billion is spent on youth sports (Wintergreen Research 2018).

The Consumers of Youth Sports

So, if youth sports are a business, who are the consumers and what is the product? The consumers are clearly the parents, and they're in a buying mood. The parents sign their children up for youth sports at increasingly early ages and are willing to spend their time and a portion of their income on sports. Organized youth sports programs now begin at very early ages, with AAU (American Athletic Union) basketball offered to under-sevens, gymnastics classes open to five-year-olds, the National Flag Football league organizing leagues for four-year-olds, Soccer Shots available to two- to three-year-olds, and Lil' Kickers available at eighteen months! And, some parents appear to be in an "arms race," where the goal is to sign their child up for sports as soon as possible and to spare no expense in pursuing their child's athletic opportunities. I remember when my daughter was four and the preschool mothers were asking me if I'd enrolled her in Kindermusic, Tumblebees, and Mommy and Me Soccer! It felt like some crazy competition among parents to demonstrate their commitment to their children by signing them up for organized activities during preschool!

In addition to starting their children in sports early, parents are also willing to pay substantial amounts of money to ensure that their children are participating in year-round sports, have access to the best coaching, gain exposure to high-level competition through travel programs, and have contact with college coaches through summer camps. Of families with children involved in youth sports, most (63 percent) spend between $1,000 and $6,000 per child per year on youth sports.

Youth sports promises outcomes that are attractive to parents, but some of these outcomes are unrealistic and sports organizations have no accountability.
Illustration by Dominy Alderman.

And you might be amazed to learn that 18 percent spend between $6,000 and $12,000, 11 percent spend between $12,000 and $24,000, and 8 percent spend more than $24,000 per child per year (Shell 2017). Think about this—for what other activities do we lay out that kind of money for our children? And these aren't just wealthy families. Some families (23 percent) have indicated that the money they are spending on youth sports is not discretionary but comes at the cost of reducing contributions to savings and retirement (Shell 2017). Clearly, the consumers have bought into the product being sold—they are willing to invest quite a bit of time and money into youth sports for their children.

The Product of Youth Sports

Let's now consider the product. What is it that youth sports organizations are selling? They are selling something that parents care about deeply: the notion that youth sports experiences are critical to the development of life skills that will lead to children becoming successful and happy adults. They are offering the alluring goal of future success, and they are specifically selling the tantalizing dreams of athletic careers for their children. Many parents have clearly bought in to the sales pitch and are committed full bore to their child's youth sports participation. Furthermore, many parents expect that the level of their financial commitment should be reflected in their child achieving successful outcomes in sports (typically defined as winning). This creates a climate that puts pressure on youth sports organizations to "win" so that parents will want to buy their product—something that you are likely to perceive as a coach.

EXAMPLE *Mission Statement*

Here is an example of what youth sports have to offer, taken from a mission statement for the WC Eagles Field Hockey Club, a youth organization: "To provide a progressive field hockey program in a challenging environment where girls and young women from the ages of 8 through 18 can train and develop to be the best players they can be. To give each player the skills, tactical understanding, vision, discipline, work ethic, decision making, and mental preparedness to play at the college level and beyond. Through the vehicle of field hockey we hope to provide each player with life skills that they will take forward into school, college, the work force, and their personal lives." This is an amazing promise that extends well beyond the child's youth sports years.

So, what parents would not do everything in their power to ensure that their child has access to all that youth sports has to offer? This desire to provide their children with every opportunity possible has then led to the arms race just described. Because parents see the chance to start their child in sports before preschool and are aware of sports programs that provide year-round training and high-level competition and the proliferation of high-dollar sports programs and boarding schools, many have come to believe that they owe it to their children to sign them up for the highest level of training as soon as possible. In other words, there is a perception that if parents do not enroll their children in sports early and make a commitment to sports as a family, they are failing their children.

The irony here is that youth sports have become more about the *parents'* goals for their children than about the experiences of the young athlete. The parents have taken the bait with respect to the products that the youth sports organizations are selling. Remember, the "products" are athletic careers and the promise that youths will develop into successful adults. But the irony is that youth sports programs are not accountable with respect to the products they have advertised. Let's look at the evidence.

With respect to an athletic career, we must understand that only a very small percentage of athletes will receive college athletic scholarships and an even smaller percentage will have the opportunity to pursue a professional career as an athlete. Out of approximately 7.3 million high school athletes, *only approximately 150,000 will receive scholarships to play sports in the National College Athletic Association (NCAA)* (Soriano and Kerr, 2019). So, the notion of playing sports in return for a paid college education is precarious at best. Furthermore, fewer than 1 percent of NCAA athletes, or 1,400 athletes of the 7.3 million high school athletes, will ultimately play their sport at a professional level (NCAA, 2019). Since the "product" of a sports career that is being sold by many youth sports organizations may be attainable for an incredibly select few young athletes, it is certainly not the most probable outcome of their sports participation. In fact, a more likely outcome for youth athletes is that they will receive an academic scholarship. *There is substantially more funding available to support academic scholarships than there is funding to support sports scholarships.* For example, at the University of Michigan, 2 percent of students are on athletic scholarships, while 70 percent are on academic scholarships (Bacon 2016). Ironically, parents in the United States are spending more money on sports skills training than they are on academic tutors or academic support for their children.

....

KEY POINT *Percentage of*
High School Athletes Playing at the Next Level

- Approximately 2 percent of high school athletes will play Division I NCAA sports.
- Fewer than 1 percent will play Division II NCAA sports.

(*Source:* National Collegiate Athletic Association 2019)

....

Perhaps most parents don't actually expect that their child will play sports collegiately or professionally. Perhaps they are focused on the promise that youth sports participation will help their child become a successful adult in career paths outside of sport. The premise here is that by participating in youth sports, children will develop life skills that will help them be successful adults. That is, our expectation is that by learning the value of hard work, demonstrating dedication, cooperating with others in team settings, exhibiting sportsmanship, and learning to accept winning and losing, our children will translate these values and skills to other settings. As the coach, you have the power to help make this happen, but it doesn't happen automatically; you have to conscientiously make the development of life skills a part of your coaching. We know that life skills are not learned simply by participating in sports. In fact, in leagues where teaching these skill sets is not specifically built into the curriculum, not all children will learn such skills to the same degree. Hence, there is no guarantee that participating in sports will help children develop skills that will have an impact on their achievements post-sports.

The wild west

One of the fascinating things to consider about youth sports is that this growing industry exists without any oversight. In fact, youth sports have been described as "the Wild West" without a sheriff (Kelley and Carchia 2013). Think about how strange this is, given our well-founded concern about anything that might affect our children. Most industries that have a direct impact on children are governed by federal-level entities. Consider the Food and Drug Administration, which is responsible for the public safety of foods and medications, or the Federal Trade Commission, which has oversight over tobacco and alcohol marketing to children. By contrast, youth sports are not governed by any federal- or state-level entity. That is to say, there are no controls related to truth in advertising or over the quality of the programs being offered by the multitude of sports programs.

Let's look at this situation from a different point of view. Aside from coaches, the other individuals who formally interact with children in sports settings are physical educators. Physical educators have years of formal collegiate-level education that includes courses on curriculum design, instructional strategies, motor development, motor learning, child development, learning, motivation, pedagogy, and child psychology. They also complete at least a semester of student teaching under the tutelage of an experienced teacher. By contrast, most sports organizations require only that volunteer youth coaches complete a criminal background check, and in some cases also require concussion or sexual harassment education. For most youth sports coaches, there is no obligation for coaching certifications, and typically the organizations do not provide any education in terms of working with children in sport. In our schools, we demand that adults who will be working with our children (teachers) are trained to do so. But in sports, we hand our children over to youth sports coaches who at most have passed a criminal background check. Such a situation emphasizes the need for this book. Obviously, it can't compare to years of formal collegiate education, but the goal in this book is to offer some key points that will help you have a positive influence on your athletes.

....

KEY POINT *Requirements to Be a Youth Sports Coach*

The only standard requirement for a youth sports coach is to pass a criminal background check.

....

Why This Matters

So, how does this knowledge that youth sports are a business, with parents as consumers and with promises of athletic careers and life skills for children, influence you in your role as coach? First, it is important for you to recognize that many parents are approaching youth sports with a consumer mind-set. They have paid for a product and expect to receive that product. Unfortunately, the premise that an early and year-round commitment to expensive youth sports is directly linked to opportunities to play at a collegiate or professional level is flawed from the outset. Furthermore, many parents somehow equate the reaching of these goals with a need to win at the youth level. They want their child to play for organizations that win and for coaches who win, and that begins to supersede their goals of character development and personal improvement. If you can help parents understand their faulty reasoning and keep their focus on personal growth, that may enable them to adopt more realistic goals for their children in sports. You do this by explaining to them that a focus on winning at all costs actually sets their child up for disappointment and failure because it is not possible for their child to win in every competition. That is, even if their child is the best athlete initially and experiences success early on, the only way to ensure winning all of the time is to compete against weaker opponents. If parents aspire for their child to play at a high level, then that means the competition level will continuously increase, making the outcomes of competition increasingly uncertain. In fact, long-term participation in sports at a high level guarantees that athletes will experience losses. If athletes care only about winning and begin to experience losses on a regular basis, their responses are likely to be very negative (for example, dropping out or feigning injuries to avoid participation). Remind parents that sports is a vehicle through which their children can learn to be gracious winners and resilient losers, can develop their abilities within their sport while learning to focus on self-improvement rather than competitive outcomes, and can mature as leaders, teammates, and friends in ways that will help them well beyond sports. By having these conversations with the parents, you will gain the freedom to coach in a developmentally appropriate way with a focus on personal growth.

Second, since most parents are also approaching sports with the expectation that their child will develop life skills that will benefit them beyond sports, it is valuable for you to be a good role model of those life skills and to integrate the development of life skills into your training (see chapter 4). Third, many children have, unfortunately, also begun to believe that winning and losing matters in youth sports. The trappings of participation (invested parents, team uniforms and gear, travel, tournaments, trophies) provide a powerful influence over their understanding of what is important. Although I recognize that it may feel like an uphill battle, as their coach *you can help your athletes set appropriate goals, learn to positively interpret the outcomes of competition, and keep sports and winning in perspective.* This will go a long way toward helping your athletes focus on what is actually important in youth sports—making friends, having fun, developing skills, and learning to love the game.

Given all of this, how are you supposed to prepare to meet the challenges that you will face? There are two bodies of knowledge that you will want to acquire to become an exceptional coach. One comprises the techniques and tactics that are required for your sport. If you have a background in the sport you are coaching, then you may bring much of that with you already. But remember that playing the game isn't the same as coaching the game. Regardless of your sports background, it will be valuable to spend time reading coaching books, looking at websites, taking advantage of coaching education opportunities, and learning various methods from other coaches to help with teaching the techniques and tactics of your sport. Ideas for practice activities can be found in abundance online and in bookstores and by watching other coaches' practices. That being said, if you are coaching at the youth level, keep in mind that there is much the athletes can gain by simply letting the game be their teacher. In other words, if you construct practices that are filled with game-related activities, young athletes will pick up some of what they need to know simply through their own problem solving within the game. Letting the game be the teacher is a great option for coaches of all levels of expertise.

KEY POINT *Drills*

Remember that some of the best athletes in the world started out playing in their backyard, in the streets, or at a park. Organized drills are not necessary to teach the game.

The second body of knowledge includes information from the areas of pedagogy (the method and practice of teaching), child development (understanding the athletes at their developmental level), and psychology (knowing how to relate to people). This book uses this body of knowledge to help you learn how to interact with your athletes in such a way as to foster their love of the game and to help them develop the life skills promised by youth sports organizations. Hence, this book is designed to help you acquire the critical skills you need to have a positive effect on your athletes.

Activity

There are two types of information you will need to be an effective coach—information related to teaching techniques and tactics and information related to ensuring that children have the best possible experience playing for you. The latter will be addressed in the remainder of this book. The former can be found in a number of places. Identify coaching education resources that are available to you.

Try these options:

1. Look at your league/club's web page for coaching resources.
2. Look for coaching clinics available near you.
3. Search for online resources related to your sport.
4. Search for books written for coaches in your sport.

CHAPTER THREE

....

The Sandlot

....

Have you ever seen the 1993 movie *The Sandlot*? If not, you should take the time to watch it. Clearly, there are some negatives portrayed in the movie, such as when the neighborhood children are unwelcoming to a new kid, Scotty, in part because he doesn't know how to play baseball. But, once the most popular boy on the team, Benny, sticks up for Scotty, the situation changes completely, and Scotty begins to be integrated into the team. What is so special about *The Sandlot* is that it provides a view of sports at its most "pure." Neighborhood kids meet at a local field to play baseball every day and at any time of day. They are not wearing uniforms, have only one ball, and wear gloves that are of questionable integrity. What you will notice right away is that there are no adults at the baseball field. In fact, the person in charge of the baseball activities is a teenage participant. This teenager's primary goal appears to be to help his friends improve so that they can provide an appropriate defensive challenge for him when he is at bat. The movie beautifully shows the joy that the children experience with small successes in the game. It reveals the skills the boys learn by working together to create expectations for their own performance, the decisions made by the children with respect to whether or not a player is safe at the base and when it is the next person's turn to bat, and the level of intrinsic motivation that is so obviously inherent in the playing of the game.

But the games that we see played in *The Sandlot* are very different from today's baseball games and practices. Baseball games now are often held on professionally manicured fields, with children wearing matching practice uniforms and carrying equipment bags with multiple

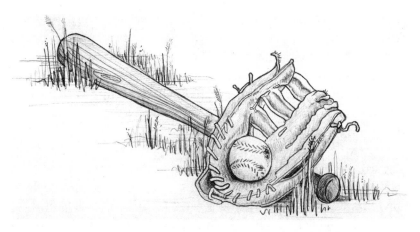

In previous eras, youth sports was more about kids than it was about adults. The competitions were organized by kids who used whatever equipment they had, created their own teams, and adapted and interpreted the rules of the game themselves.
Illustration by Dominy Alderman.

bats and batting gloves, coaches providing instruction, and parents in attendance to offer their own feedback during and after the game. Now, the trappings of the game are beautiful, but I would argue that the game itself is not as inherently beautiful. This is in part because the experience that the youth athletes have in sports is now largely under the control of the coaches and the parents who provide this structured environment, where children do not have the same level of input as they did in days of old. Youth sports today are commercial entities and a by-product of the proliferation of suburbs and safety concerns that result in us being afraid to allow children to be out on their own. I say this not to imply that this fear is unfounded but rather to point out that the side effect is that children do not have the same opportunities as they once did to interact with others in free-play situations.

The distinction between today's youth sports and youth sports from decades ago is an important one, particularly as it relates to the goal of developing life skills in young athletes. Again, think back to the baseball games depicted in *The Sandlot*. In those games, children have opportunities to make their own decisions regarding the rules, the teams, playing positions, and batting orders. They argue about the rules and then are forced to come to consensus so the games can continue. They are given the chance for their leadership, communication, and negotiation skills to emerge and develop. Contrast that with today's youth sports, which are completely adult-driven. The league organizers have decided on the rules, the coaches make the decisions regarding playing positions and batting orders, and the umpires tell us whether a ball is fair or foul and whether the player is safe or out. Where in this scenario are the kids getting any chance to develop their own life skills? How are they learning to be "good people" through their sports experiences? How are they acquiring the strength of character promised to the parents by the sports organization? Unfortunately, most children are not getting these opportunities within their sports experience, and as a result, they are not reaping the potential benefits that sports have to offer in terms of character development. This is where coaches come in. Although you can't roll the clock back to days of old when children could engage in free play on their own, you can help to engender the development of life skills into your coaching. You have the opportunity to infuse character development into your sessions, to model appropriate behavior, and to reward demonstrations of leadership, hard work, and ethical decision-making. This is one of the most important responsibilities you have as a coach of young athletes. In addition to this, you have the capacity to teach the youth athletes correct motor skills, strategy and tactics, and sportsmanship. You can add your game-related expertise to the youth sports experience and can lead your practices and games in ways that foster the development of the athletes as young people.

....

KEY POINT *The Coach's Responsibilities*

You are largely responsible for the athletes' sports experience. You have the awesome opportunity to contribute to their development as athletes and as people. Ironically, to do this, you will have to let go of some of your control. Give your athletes opportunities to develop as leaders and to work autonomously to improve in their sports. Help them reach their potential by focusing on their development not just as athletes but as young people. Cherish them and put their well-being and personal development above all else.

....

Mission Statements

A mission statement is a formal written explanation of the aims and values of an organization. In youth sports, the mission statement shares the big-picture philosophy for the sports club. Some sports organizations also have vision statements describing the ultimate outcomes for the organization and core values that identify the behaviors they want to reinforce. Youth sports organizations that are focused primarily on youth development often include all three of these (a mission statement, a vision, and core values). You can find examples with national organizations like Girls on the Run (https://www.girlsontherun.org/Who -We-Are/Our-Mission) and the First Tee (https://thefirsttee.org/about/). Take a moment to look up the mission statement for the youth sports organization you are working with. Write down key words from the mission statement for your organization.

_____

_____

_____

Now let's see how those key words compare to those we find if we look at the mission statements for most popular sports in the United States (basketball, soccer, baseball/softball, football, gymnastics, track and field, volleyball). I have created a word cloud based upon mission statements from these sports (see fig. 3.1).

KEY COMPONENTS OF MISSION STATEMENTS

In the word cloud, larger font sizes identify words that appear the most in the mission statements I consulted. Hence, the common terms across this wide variety of sports are "teamwork," "competitive," "respect," "sportsmanship," "character," "safe," and "skills." Clearly, youth sports organizations engaged in wide variety of sports and from across the country are consistent in their stated goals of developing sport-related skills and life skills in athletes in their programs. How do these mission statements compare with the mission statement you found for your organization?

Figure 3.1. Word cloud showing terms commonly included in the mission statements of a variety of youth sports organizations. Image created using www.wordclouds.com.

In general, these mission statements make sense when we consider that the key words represent the products that the youth sports organizations are "selling" to parents as they promote their clubs and programs to their target consumers. If parents are trying to find information about a local sports program online, one of the very first things they will see on the organization's website is likely to be the mission statement. These mission statements support the idea that youth sports are focused on the development of life skills.

So, the next question we must consider is how the sports organizations are making sure that these life skills are developed. I encourage you to check with your own sports organization. You can look at your organization's website or speak to the program directors or other coaches in the organization to ask them what steps they are taking, what curriculum they are using, or what aspects of the program are specifically designed to help achieve the goals identified in their mission statement. Assuming that life skills are one of the organization's goals, you could ask them how they assess whether they are meeting (or failing to meet) their goals. Now, if you've ever thought about this before or if you start asking these questions, you might be laughing with me as you read this, because it is unlikely you will get any information about your organization's methods of assessment. And unfortunately, it is likely that the folks you question will quickly become defensive, and the conversation may end up being pretty short.

The reason that you are not likely to get very far pursuing this line of conversation with your sports organization is that there are very few organizations that actually have a curriculum, league rules, coaching education, or anything else in place to formally work to meet the life-development goals identified in the mission statement. And fewer still have ever actually done anything to assess the extent to which life skills are developed through their programs. The exceptions are those sports organizations such as First Tee and Girls on the Run, which were explicitly designed to develop young people in terms of character and life skills. Other than those types of programs, it appears that most of the youth sports organizations and the parents who join them are under the impression that these life skills will develop automatically and that they are guaranteed outcomes of participation. In other words, the assumption seems to be that all a child has to do is to participate in youth sports, and life skills will develop.

Although this assumption is certainly debatable, it might have been accurate in the days of *The Sandlot*, where children were in charge and the lack of an adult presence provided an environment where the problem-solving and concomitant character development were under the athletes' control. And there is a growing movement in support of giving children opportunities for free play (Iannelli 2017). But in today's youth sports and in the absence of a specific character-building curriculum, there is actually evidence that young athletes are *not* developing these life skills through sport. In fact, some evidence shows that sports may not always help and sometimes may hinder moral reasoning (that is, the ability to determine what is right and wrong in a specific situation). For example, there is evidence showing that sports participants and nonparticipants exhibit equivalent levels of moral reasoning (suggesting that sports do not inherently improve young athletes' abilities to make good choices). And in fact, moral reasoning has been found to be lower for male contact sports participants as compared to nonparticipants (Gould and Carson 2008), indicating that male contact sports may actually "teach" athletes to make bad moral decisions.

WHAT MISSION STATEMENTS DON'T SAY

Several characteristics of youth sports organizations are not explicitly identified in the mission statements but are evident from the structure of the organizations. One obvious goal of youth sports appears to be talent identification, with the resulting devotion of resources to the development of the "top" athletes. This is evident from the fact that in many organizations, there are different levels of competition at each age group. In fact, a soccer club near my community now identifies the top twenty-two to twenty-six players in the under-eleven age group to be on its top team. This team plays twenty-eight to thirty games per season and practices four days a week, and athletes are not allowed to play for their school teams. The club then identifies a second level below that and goes on to rank-order the teams in the third level of competitive play. This degree of ranking of athletes is being done by the sports organization despite the fact that it is very difficult to identify talent in young children. Remember, this is done with U11 (under eleven years old) players who have not even approached puberty, making talent identification by youth sports coaches particularly challenging. An additional challenge of identifying the most talented athletes at early ages is that most sports use one-year age ranges, which disadvantage children with late birthdates. Think about it—there are huge differences between a child who has just turned ten and a child who is ten years and eleven months old, yet these children will be judged and compared to one another, which has implications for their opportunities for success in sports. Clearly, the older athletes have the advantage, which can then result in them getting more opportunities than the younger athletes.

In fact, there are numerous studies that clearly demonstrate the advantage that those with an earlier birth month have over those with a later birth month. This is called the relative age effect and is most evident in children eleven years old and younger but remains evident in twelve- to fourteen-year-olds to a greater extent than is seen in fifteen- to nineteen-year-olds. It has been demonstrated in recreational-level through elite adult-level athletes and is strongest in elite sports for twelve- to fourteen-year-olds (Smith et al. 2018).

KEY POINT *Identifying the Most Talented Athletes*

Even experts are accurate only about 50 percent of the time when it comes to identifying players who will be successful at higher levels and those who will not. That is, essentially a coin toss determines which athletes get access to the best resources.

Despite our knowledge that top-level players *cannot* be identified at early ages and the evidence that birth month has an impact on the ability level of athletes, club programs purport to be able to identify the more talented players at early ages and then are devoting better coaches and extra resources to these athletes (Gladwell 2008). This feeds right into the parents' beliefs that sports provide a training ground for their child to advance to elite status and encourages them to invest their time and money into these more expensive programs.

The reality of youth sports is that most organizations are designed to develop talented players at the expense of less skillful athletes. This is a mistake for many reasons, including that talent identification is not a perfect science, that the equal distribution of resources would benefit all athletes, and that all youth athletes should be developed to reach their potential. Project Play is an initiative of the Aspen Institute Sports and Society Program that is working to promote the development of healthy communities through youth sports. Project Play has produced reports that share views of the problems and the solutions to help youth sports today. In their problems section, they provide a depiction of a youth sports model that they describe as being "broken." Figure 3.2 depicts the progression of the most skilled athletes through the increasingly more selective levels. It also shows how those who do not fit this description

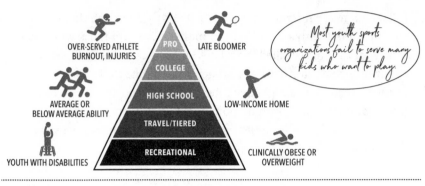

OVER-SERVED ATHLETE BURNOUT, INJURIES

LATE BLOOMER

PRO

COLLEGE

HIGH SCHOOL

AVERAGE OR BELOW AVERAGE ABILITY

LOW-INCOME HOME

TRAVEL/TIERED

RECREATIONAL

YOUTH WITH DISABILITIES

CLINICALLY OBESE OR OVERWEIGHT

Most youth sports organizations fail to serve many kids who want to play.

TOTAL POPULATION

Figure 3.2. Many youth sports organizations are purposefully designed to exclude participants along each step of the way. As a result, the organizations fail to serve large groups of children who would like to be engaged in organized sports. Figure adapted with permission from the Aspen Institute, Project Play, http://youthreport.projectplay.us/the-problem.

are not a part of the youth sports model at all (unless they choose to stay at recreational levels, which tend to decrease in availability with advancing age).

What you will notice is that as you move up the triangle, the number of individuals involved at each level of play progressively decreases. And the individuals who are on the outside of the pyramid are not even a part of the equation. As players move up this pyramid, the "more talented" children have opportunities to move to higher levels of competition, which results in access to better coaching, higher-quality facilities, and more travel. The result is that many children drop out because they either have not been selected for higher level teams, do not have the requisite financial resources, or are no longer having fun as the demands increase and the opportunities to stay with their friends decrease.

The unintended consequence of the "broken" model of youth sports is the reduction in the number of children participating in youth sports. The irony of this is that it doesn't seem consistent with a business model. From a business perspective, wouldn't it make sense to keep as many people involved in your sport as long as you could? In theory, sports programs, leagues, and coaching education should be designed in a way that helps youth sports participants fall in love with the game to the extent that they would want to continue playing, even into adulthood. In that way, the business model of sports would benefit

Up to age 12, focus on ability, confidence, and desire to be active.

Squaring the pyramid creates athletes for life, at all levels.

Figure 3.3. Youth sports organizations should provide opportunities to anyone who is interested in participating, regardless of ability or age. This would result in larger numbers of participants and could contribute to a healthier nation. Figure adapted with permission from the Aspen Institute, Project Play, http://youthreport.projectplay.us/the-solution/.

from lifelong participation! This would be wonderful because the numbers of participants in the bottom-most level would stay the same into adulthood as a result of the development of a lifelong love of physical activity. Instead of a pyramid, we would have a column with relatively equal numbers at every level. As illustrated in figure 3.3, we could use our physical education and youth sports programs to develop physical literacy in all participants. This would then ensure that there were recreational opportunities available in all sports, which would provide opportunities for large numbers of children to stay engaged with sports through adolescence and, ideally, into adulthood. Can you imagine the positive health impact this would have on our entire nation? Sadly, this isn't the model that youth sports are using, in large part because they are competing for youth athletes who want to be a part of a winning club. Thus youth sports organizations recruit large numbers of children at the lower levels and use these large numbers and increasing costs at higher levels of play to support their business model.

Clearly, the most depressing thing from a health perspective and from a societal viewpoint is that this model moves children out of youth sports in a systematic way such that most children are not playing organized sports by the time they are teenagers. Youth sports have fallen into their own trap of purporting to develop elite-level athletes and selling that as their product. I imagine it would be difficult to sell the promise of remaining at a level of recreational play into adulthood, despite this idea of a healthy lifestyle being in the best interest of our children and our society. Wouldn't it be great if there was a movement toward sports being about participation by all, from childhood through adulthood? As youth sports currently exist, we are not meeting goals related to helping children develop active lifestyles, and we are certainly missing opportunities to provide a positive sports experience for these young people.

....

KEY POINT *A Different Vision of Sports*

Wouldn't it be cool if

- it was normal to see adults playing team sports?
- you saw women playing pickup basketball?
- you saw parents and their kids playing tennis?
- you saw families out walking together?

....

Why This Matters

Think back to what you wrote as your reasons for coaching. Clearly, you have a role to play in keeping children involved in sports and physical activity by helping them develop an intrinsic love of the game. You also have a role to play in terms of helping to ensure that their sports experience is a vehicle for the development of physical activity and life skills that they will carry with them into adulthood. But it is important for you to recognize that there are forces at play that are influencing your athletes' experience in sports and that run counter to these lofty goals. These influences include the portrayal of sports in the media; the athlete's parents, siblings, and peers; the sports organization itself; and society at large. The focus of youth sports is misplaced, and we really need to regain the correct focus to help improve the experiences of youth athletes.

Let me give you an example designed to get you to think about your own focus in youth sports. Imagine that your child just came home from a sporting event and you didn't get to see him or her play. What is the first question you would ask?

_____

_____

My guess is that you wrote, "Did you win?" And actually, for many adults, that is the only question they ask, and once they have the answer, the conversation is over. Now, let's examine this question for a minute. What does it imply? It implies that we believe the outcome of the event is the most important thing. In fact, if there are no follow-up questions, it tells athletes that the outcome is the *only* thing that matters. The question also implies that we believe that winning was in their control. And it suggests that we care less (or not at all) about other things like having fun, trying their hardest, and showing good sportsmanship. How did that happen? How did we go from our mission statement and our goals, which are focused on having fun, learning to love the game, and developing life skills, to asking only about winning? It's a common occurrence for people surrounding a young athlete to behave and speak in ways suggesting that all they care about is winning.

The ironic thing for me personally is that I have been asking my children a different question for years and am still struggling to combat the external influences on them. One day, my son came home from a baseball game that I could not attend. When he got home, I asked him, "How was the game?" He replied, "We lost." I said, "You know I don't care about winning or losing. How was the game?" After some thought, my son said, "Well, I played okay. The other team was really big, strong, and aggressive. I think Durrell needs new glasses." It's interesting, isn't it? My son answered my question with a statement about winning and losing even though he has to know (because I've been telling him for years) that I don't care about that. When he's pressed to go beyond the outcome of the game, the answers I get typically still revolve around his performance and the performance of his teammates. I have to ask a third time to find out "Well, did you have fun? Did you try hard? Did you or anyone on your team do anything positive in the game? Did you try any new skills? Was anybody a really good sport?" These are the questions that really matter. If my child says "Yes" to these questions, then why in the world would I care if he won or lost? Remember, this is youth sports. This isn't Wimbledon or the World Series or the World Cup. Winning matters only to the extent that we allow it to matter. We can make it the most important part of their participation, or we can make sure that we keep winning and losing in perspective. If winning and losing become the reason the athletes are playing, then no wonder we lose kids from youth sports in huge numbers, because guess what? In every competition, only one team or player can be the winner. Everyone can have fun, everyone can improve, and everyone can get joy from trying their hardest, but not everyone can win. And if winning is all that matters, then we quickly and dramatically reduce the number of people who want to participate in sports.

....

KEY POINT *Winning and Losing*

- In games where winning is determined by the score, at least half of the participants will lose.
- In games where an athletes' improvement and playing their best is what matters, everyone can win.

....

So, back to your role as the coach. You can ensure that your athletes have fun by helping them focus on the aspects of the game that are in their control. You can help your athletes to derive satisfaction from trying hard. You can help them recognize good play and sportsmanship by their teammates and their opponents. You can help them keep winning in perspective. You can reward good decisions, hard work, and persistence. And if you do these things, then you are going to be a great coach because you are going to have a positive impact on your athletes and are going to help them develop a love for the game and the skills they will need to contribute to success in sports and beyond. It will be a struggle because you are up against many other forces intent on winning, but I have confidence that you can make a difference.

Activity

Look back at the mission statement for your sports organization. (If your organization doesn't have one, write down some key words that you think are important in terms of the development of your athletes.) Identify three ways that you can help your athletes to attain these important goals. In other words, provide your own coaching mission statement (or philosophy) that explains what your goals are in working with your athletes.

Example: By reinforcing good sportsmanship, I will enhance the athletes' moral development (that is, knowing right from wrong).

1. _____

2. _____

3. _____

4. _____

5. _____

6. _____

CHAPTER FOUR

....

Coaches as Teachers

....

One of your primary goals as a coach should be to be a great teacher. When you think of the necessary skill sets to be a great coach, you will notice that they overlap substantially with the skill sets of great teachers. Great teachers increase their students' understanding of their content area while also imbuing in them a love for that topic. You can tell that someone is a *really great* teacher if they can make their students love topics that might not be inherently enjoyable. As an example, I know that my children have a *really great* Latin teacher because they are learning Latin and are also telling me that they love Latin! To me, that is a huge compliment to the teacher because she is taking a topic that might not be intrinsically motivating (apologies to classics fans!) and making it fun. In a sport, this should be easy because the sport itself is inherently fun. We recognize that the best coaches have knowledge of the technical skills and the tactical skills that are relevant to the sport, but we should also recognize that great coaches also know how to communicate their knowledge to the athletes in ways that increase their motivation for the sport. In other words, having content knowledge of a sport is not enough. As a coach, you must also be able to share this knowledge effectively and in a way that makes the experience enjoyable to the athletes. One key to this is to use good communication skills. Through good communication skills, you can deliver relevant knowledge, information, and advice while also fostering intrinsic motivation. Of course you have to teach the technical and tactical aspects of your sport, but if you are a great coach, you will do that in an enjoyable way that makes the athletes love the sport and yearn for your input. To be a great coach, you must be a teacher of the sport who understands the personalities of the athletes in a way that allows you to be able to relate well to each and every one of them.

....

KEY POINT *Steiner's Model*

Potential productivity
 – Losses due to faulty individual processes
 – Losses due to faulty group processes
 _____

= Actual productivity

(*Source*: Steiner 1966)

....

To illustrate the importance of communication skills and effective coaching, let's think about a silly example from perhaps one of the simplest team contests: tug-of-war. Tug-of-war is a competitive event that should be determined by the sum of the strength of the members of one side in comparison to the sum of the strength of the members of the other side. So in theory, the competition itself seems unnecessary because the outcome should be a foregone conclusion. If Team A has five athletes who can each pull at a force of 100 pounds ($5 \times 100 = 500$ pounds) and Team B has five athletes who can each pull at a force of 110 pounds ($5 \times 110 = 550$ pounds), then it seems clear that Team B will be the victor. No coach required! However, even in an activity as simple as tug-of-war, there are important considerations that determine the extent to which the potential performance (in this case, 550 pounds of force) matches the actual performance (see Steiner's model below). Actual performance will equal potential performance only if the athletes are giving 100 percent effort and working together. At the individual level, if there is a lack of motivation, a failure in technique, a lack of preparedness, fatigue, or injury, the athlete will not perform at his or her best. At the team level, if there is a deficiency in coordination, a lack of proper tactics, or miscommunication among teammates, the team will not perform at its best. The job of the coach is to maximize the individual athlete's ability to perform at his or her best and the team's ability to reach its potential. In this tug-of-war example, the individual-based ways to do that would be to ensure that each athlete has a firm grip on the rope, good body position, and appropriate footwear. The team-based ways to do this would include making sure that the athletes all pull their hardest at the same time and that they are strategically placed along the rope to most benefit the team. Regarding motivation, it is critical that you get the athletes to give their best so that they perform as close as possible to their maximum ability. By doing these things, you help the team reach their potential of 550 pounds of force.

In a more general sense, effective coaches have several skill sets that contribute to their ability to get the most from their team. The coach must be a good teacher—sharing knowledge regarding techniques and tactics and providing feedback in a way that helps athletes improve their performance. The coach must also be a good motivator, possessing the necessary interpersonal skills to reach each of the athletes at that moment in time. Let's talk about these skills in more detail.

Being a Good Teacher

You can undoubtedly think back to times when you have had a teacher who was excellent and a teacher who was not as effective. Consider the characteristics of the excellent teacher—this is the person who increased your enthusiasm for the subject matter, who helped you learn the subject matter relative to your current level of knowledge, and who rewarded your efforts and encouraged you to work hard. These same characteristics are evident in coaches who are effective. At its heart, a coach's job is to be an excellent teacher in the specific subject of the sport.

A lot goes into being an effective teacher, but let me share some specific thoughts that relate to coaching. First, it is important that you design each of your practices and the structure of your practices across the season with a specific plan in place. Each practice should have *learning objectives* that are supported by the activities the athletes will be asked to perform. Prior to the practice, spend some time considering what it is that you want the athletes to get out of that practice and then design activities that lead to that goal. And the practices should have a flow that makes sense across the course of the season (or the preseason). For example, in team sports like basketball, soccer, hockey, lacrosse, and field hockey, if you are working with relatively novice athletes, it doesn't make sense to focus a practice on shooting and defending before you have taught more personal skills that involve controlling the ball or puck. Early in the season, you would likely focus on these personal skills and then build up to passing/receiving, shooting, and defense. If you

Prior to each practice, coaches should identify learning
objectives and create a progression of activities designed
to help their athletes reach those objectives.
Illustration by Dominy Alderman.

are working with a more experienced team, you might be able to use
the personal skills as part of your warm-up and then get into activities
that focus on passing/receiving earlier in the season.

Within the practice itself, *include warm-up activities* (that incorporate the learning objectives as much as possible) and then *build from
relatively simple activities* (like two people passing back and forth) *to more
complex activities* (like four people passing with light defensive pressure). When moving from simple to complex in team sports, increase
the numbers of players, decrease time and space, and/or increase defensive pressure (in that order). In individual or coactive sports (like tennis
or golf), do this in a parallel fashion by adding the demands on the
players so that they learn to perform in progressively higher-pressure
scenarios. For example, tennis players might first hit a ball while sta-
tionary, then hit a ball while moving in a predetermined direction, and
then hit a ball delivered to unpredictable locations. This sequence of

events allows for success while also gradually increasing the demands on the athletes with a goal of preparing them for real-world situations.

During the practice, you should also watch to identify teachable moments. If you offer instruction constantly, the extent to which your athletes actually listen to you will wear off. In addition, you will not be preparing them to perform in situations when you are not present or where your instructions cannot be delivered because of team rules, logistics, speed of play, or other reasons. Instead, look for opportunities to provide instruction on a regular (but not constant) basis. When you see something that could be improved, stop play immediately so that the athletes will recognize the error. Use a sandwich approach by offering a positive comment, pointing out the error, asking them to describe the solution, and then clarifying what you would like to see and offering encouragement. By instructing them in this fashion, you help them learn to problem-solve on their own, which increases their ability to perform independently in their sport. Once the solution is understood, restart play so that they have the opportunity to correct their performance before continuing.

If you have situations where you are not achieving your goals in a practice, be sure to ask yourself what the reason is. Is it because the activity is not understood? Is it because something about the structure of the activity is not right (for instance, the space is too big or you need to add a rule to help create the behavior that you want to see)? If you identify any of these problems, don't be afraid to adjust the activity midstream to help achieve your goals. In my opinion, this is the true sign of a masterful coach—not necessarily because the activities are perfect right away (although this may come with experience) but rather because the coach can adjust the activity spontaneously when the desired outcomes are not observed. For example, imagine that you have designed an activity in which you want to see players looking for opportunities to score but observe that the players are passing one or two times more than necessary and there are numerous turnovers as a result. Obviously, you can stop play at teachable moments to encourage the shot, but maybe that's not all that is necessary. Maybe instead you want to reduce the number of defenders by one, to reward shots taken but not made with a point system, or to limit the number of passes or touches to encourage quicker shot-taking. As the coach, don't be afraid to stop and adjust your activity to achieve the desired objectives.

If you have situations where you are losing the athletes' attention, be sure to think about why this could be. If it appears that several athletes have lost their focus, then the responsibility is clearly yours. I can't tell you how many practices I have watched where the activity itself is boring, includes too many inactive athletes, or goes on for too long. It is not surprising that in these situations, athletes at the back of the line or who are not engaged in the activity or who are simply bored begin to lose their focus and sometimes even become disruptive. When this happens, it is disheartening to see coaches berate or punish their athletes for their failure to pay attention. In fact, the coach should be chastised for not paying attention to the activity, not recognizing the body language of the players, and not making the necessary adjustments to ensure that the athletes stay focused. If you are the coach and you observe that several athletes are not paying attention, you should immediately make an adjustment to the activity or take a break so that the athletes can regain their focus. Be self-reflective. Has the activity gone on too long? Is the activity not understood? Is the activity boring? Are there are too many inactive athletes during the activity? Once you identify the reason for the problem, make an appropriate adjustment to pull the athletes back into your practice.

The situations discussed above refer to times when you have several athletes who are not paying attention. But it may be that you have one or two athletes who consistently have trouble with this. If this is the case, be sure to talk with the athlete and/or the athlete's parents to make sure you understand the reason. Maybe the athlete is fatigued, maybe he has attention deficit disorder and is not on his medication, or maybe he has something else going on that has him distracted. Importantly, if you feel that you need to discipline the athlete to help him keep his focus, be sure that the disciplinary action you choose is consistent with your overall goals and that it doesn't make matters worse. In other words, if you want the athlete to focus on the activity at hand, consider simply asking him to focus rather than pulling him out of the activity. Think about giving the athlete a more engaged role in the activity to help him keep his focus. Be creative in how you work to keep all of your athletes engaged and active in your practices because this is what will result in them having the greatest enjoyment. As a minor point, remember also that if you are disciplining athletes, the discipline should not put a negative spin on the sport itself. For example, if you are coaching track and you want the athletes to help pick up any trash or lost items after a home track meet, don't tell them that they will have to run extra for anything not picked up. This makes no sense because it is actually using the sport itself (which you want them to love) as a punishment. Instead, think about other ways of encouraging or discouraging particular behaviors that serve to reinforce the positive aspects of your sport.

KEY POINT *Limit the Time You Spend Talking*

Don't talk so much that you start to sound like Charlie Brown's teacher:

Wah wah waaaah wah. Wah wah wah waaah wah.

A good rule of thumb is to talk no more than three minutes at any given time.

Another important aspect of being a good teacher is understanding how to teach motor skills and team tactics. Providing athletes with chances to perform multiple repetitions of a given movement or action and being able to offer usable feedback is key to helping them develop their motor skills. Remember that one goal for you as the coach is to ensure that the athletes get as many repetitions as possible during practices. Doing this will require some creativity on your part and may also require that you be willing to not be in control of every athlete's every movement at all times. As a great example from basketball, I have seen coaches, when working on shooting with young players, set up two lines. Those in one line are asked to dribble in a bit and then take a shot. Those in the other line rebound and get the ball to the next person in the shooting line. I've seen this activity done with sixteen kids taking turns shooting on one basket. This comes back again to the problem with lines. In this activity, only one out of sixteen kids is getting the chance to shoot at a time. Why??? If the coach has two other baskets that can be used on half of a gym, he or she should split the groups up into three smaller groups. Of course, the coach can't then give feedback to every kid on every shot, but that's not really the point. The coach can still give feedback to one group at a time while ensuring that the kids get lots of repetitions. If you find that you don't have additional baskets, then be creative. Use masking tape to mark a target on the wall and ask kids to set their feet, get their balance, and shoot the ball toward the target. No, it's not exactly the same as shooting at a basket, but the process is, and that's what you are trying to get repetitions of.

A further way to ensure that players get the greatest number of repetitions is to minimize the amount of time you spend talking or explaining activities and get them going as soon as possible. In fact, a good rule of thumb is to spend no more than three minutes describing an activity to the athletes. If explaining an activity takes longer than that, it is likely that the activity is too complex for your athletes at this time. You can also make your instruction more efficient by including a demonstration of the technique you are teaching or of the activity as you'd like it to be performed. Ask one or more of your more skillful athletes to demonstrate the behavior or the activity. Repeat the demonstration a few times, and if it isn't perfect, point out the positive aspects to the observers and comment on the places where improvement is needed. Once the activity has been demonstrated, get everybody involved as quickly as possible. Then stay quiet. Give the athletes a chance to try out the activity themselves. Let them problem solve to figure out how to improve in the activity. When you stop play at a teachable moment, be succinct. Let them know what you're seeing and what you want to see. Start play again from that point so they can perform the behavior as you've instructed. Then let play continue.

As the athletes are performing, provide both positive and critical feedback. If you see them performing the activity properly, be specific in saying what you see that is good. It isn't particularly helpful to say, "Good job." It *is* very helpful to say, "Good job, I like how you're shifting the weight from your back foot to your front foot as you swing." If you see them making a mistake in their performance, again, be specific in the feedback you give. It doesn't help to say, "Stop popping the ball up," or "Concentrate and hit the ball." Instead, use the sandwich technique to provide a specific point of instruction. Sandwich the key point between a compliment and a solution with encouragement. So, for example, you could say, "Great work shifting your weight [compliment]. But you're dropping the bat too low [key point; critique]. Concentrate on keeping the bat level through the swing [solution]. Now let's see you take a good cut [encouragement]." The athlete can then use this type of specific feedback to improve his or her technique.

KEY POINT *How to Give Feedback*

- "Good job" doesn't provide information that is specific enough. It merely tells the athletes you're happy with them.
- "Don't do that" is not specific enough. This statement tells the athletes you're not happy with them but doesn't tell them what to do so that you will be happy with them.
- If you want the athletes to change their behavior, tell them precisely what you want them to do!
- Sandwich your directive or critical feedback between a compliment and a solution with encouragement.
- Be sure to stay positive in offering feedback, and acknowledge athletes' efforts rather than just focusing on the outcome of their performance.

Another important aspect of the education environment that is partially under your control as the coach is the development of cohesion. When a group of athletes are high on cohesion, that means that everyone is on the same page in terms of their goals. Cohesion helps lead to better levels of performance, which then leads to higher levels of task cohesion in a positive cycle. You can help your team develop cohesion in several ways. One important idea is to provide opportunities for the athletes to get to know one another. If you allow athletes to self-select partners or small groups for activities, notice whether the same groups are always forming. If this is the case, you may want to mix things up a bit. One strategy is to have them identify something they have in common (for instance, tell them to find a partner who has the same number of siblings or who has the same number of pets). This is a great tactic because not only does it help create new partnerships or groups but also it provides ways for them to get to know one another better and to perhaps identify commonalities that lead to friendships.

You can also build cohesion by helping the athletes recognize each other's value and that each of them has strengths that go beyond the sport. One way to do this is by participating in an activity together outside of practices and competitions. This could be a sport-related activity, like going together to a high school, college, or professional competition. Or, it could be completely independent from sport, like having pizza and movie night, camping out in a backyard, or doing a community service project. Any of these activities can lead to opportunities to find out more about each other outside of sports. For instance, maybe I learn that one of my teammates also loves the Avengers and we have the same favorite Marvel superhero. Or, maybe I discover that one of my teammates knows how to pitch a tent. This can help a team become more cohesive, which can help athletes with their overall sports experience.

Being a Good Communicator

Are you an effective communicator? Communication is a skill that has to be practiced and refined to be most effective. When we think of communication, sometimes we focus only on the delivery of information. But it is important to remember that communication includes both the transmission and reception of that information. If a delivered message is not received as intended, then the communication has failed. The people whom you need to communicate with as the coach make up a fairly long list. You will be communicating with the athletes of course, but also with parents, other coaches, officials, league or tournament representatives, facilities managers, and athletic trainers.

At its most basic, being a good communicator requires that the information you share is properly understood by the athletes. The athlete must understand your lingo! Each sport has its own specific language that may need to be explained or shared with all the athletes (particularly those who might be relatively new to the sport or the team). If the athletes don't understand what you are saying, obviously they won't be able to respond appropriately. Examples of unique language include telling a baseball team to defend the bunt, telling a soccer team to play a flat back four, telling a basketball team to play a box-in-one, or telling your volleyball team to do a two set. Be sure to check for understanding when you call for technical or tactical adjustments and to offer clear explanations as necessary. It is important to also be sure that the athletes are communicating with one another clearly and appropriately. This can be tricky because while this communication is critical to success (particularly in team sports), it can also be challenging because of the nature of peer-to-peer interactions. You will likely have to teach your athletes how to communicate with one another effectively and appropriately. You should encourage athletes to communicate relevant information to one another and to offer positive feedback during practices and competitions. This affirmation from teammates is a big contributor to the overall sports experience. So, be sure to reinforce times when you see an athlete giving positive feedback to a teammate. At the same time, be sure to offer a correction if an athlete is being too negative or critical with a teammate. When you see or hear this happening, it is important to step in to teach the players how to interact positively with one another. I recently observed Don, a 12-year old boy, berating his teammate during a game. In close proximity to his teammate, he yelled, "What are you doing? That was a horrible shot! You shouldn't ever shoot again!" Clearly, it is important for the coach to intervene in this situation to reassure the shooter that it's okay to shoot and that it's okay if some of the shots are poor. It is equally important to explain to Don that it is not his place to judge the skill levels of his teammates or the quality of their performances. His role is to be supportive of his teammates and to focus on his own behavior, effort, and performance.

Other vitally important aspects of communication that we often don't pay as much attention to are the paraverbal and nonverbal information that is transmitted. It is important that you match what you are saying with how you look and your tone of voice. Paraverbal communication is the tone of voice and the use of inflections. Nonverbal communication is defined by body language—your posture, your facial expressions, your hand gestures. The critical point to remember is that the person you are trying to communicate with is taking in all of these aspects of your communication. If your words and your paraverbal and nonverbal communication are consistent, this will help ensure that the receiver correctly interprets your intentions. But if they are not consistent, the receiver will be left confused about your actual intent. Think about the way in which you say these things, your inflections, and your body language can be used to convey very different messages. Here is an example to clarify my point:

In response to each of the examples of coaches' possible behaviors below, consider how the athlete will react and what he or she will think. The coach pulls the athlete out of the event and says, "You played a great game." While saying this, the coach

1. Looks the athlete in the eye and gives her a fist bump.
2. Does not make eye contact with the athlete but stays focused on the game.

3. Looks over at the bench while speaking and makes eye contact with a different player.

Clearly, these three scenarios are meant to convey very different information. In the first case, the coach's comment and behaviors are consistent. The athlete feels confident that the coach is being sincere and feels proud of her contributions. She believes that she has come out of the game for tactical reasons and is comfortable with her performance. In the second case, the coach says the same thing, but seems disinterested. The athlete is probably left wondering whether the statement is sincere. She is asking herself why she was pulled from the game if she was playing a great game. She is wondering whether she did well or did poorly and is uncertain as to what the coach really thinks. In the third case, the coach is working hard to undo team cohesion! The coach appears to be complimenting the player who came off but seems to be using this as a way to make a point to a different player who is on the bench. The player who has just come off is probably uncertain about the coach's sincerity and the extent to which the coach cares about her performance at all. Meanwhile, the player on the bench knows the coach is not happy with her but may not know the specific reason or what steps she can take to get back into the coach's favor.

The key point here is that you should be very aware of your verbal, paraverbal, and nonverbal communication and should work hard to ensure that the three are consistent in conveying the message you want to transmit. When they are not consistent, the receiver of the message will feel uncertain and may or may not interpret your words correctly. In the interest of developing team cohesion, it is good to be straightforward in your communication styles and to not use communication in a way that will be perceived as manipulative, unclear, or passive-aggressive. Remember, the goal with communication is to provide a clear and consistent message to the intended recipient so she understands how to interpret the message.

Another relatively minor point about communication is to remember to *speak in positives* rather than in negatives. In other words, tell the athletes what you want them to do rather than what you don't want them to do. When you tell them what *not* to do, there are two problems. First, because of the way that people's brains work, they tend to hear the action part of a statement rather than catch that the statement has been turned negative. It's like if you tell your dog, "I'm sorry, we are not going for a walk today." As soon as you say that, your dog is likely to run to find his leash; bring it back, tail wagging; and be ready to go. The dog didn't hear the word "not," and neither will your athletes. The second problem is that by telling them what *not* to do, you have not given them any guidance as to what *to do*, and there are limitless options as to what to do. So, as a very simple example, if you tell your players, "Don't miss," their focus will be on the word "miss," and they have no idea what they need to do to ensure that they "don't miss." It's amazing how often we'll hear this guidance during a competition—"Don't miss," "Don't shoot high," "Don't overcorrect," "Don't double-fault," "Don't stab at the ball," "Don't drop your elbow." The list goes on and on! As a coach, your task is to provide one or two pointers that help the athletes focus on what they should do in specific terms. So, you might say, "Concentrate on your footwork to be in a good position," or, "Take a good first touch and get your head up to find your teammates."

The last important point about communication is to remember that it is meant to be a two-way street. As the coach, it is critical that you welcome input from your athletes, that you offer them opportunities to express their thoughts and feelings, and that you are an active listener who is in tune with the team. This is part of positive coaching. As you develop practices and handle competitions in a way that is reflective of positive coaching, you will want to invite input from your athletes. Simply ask for their ideas on a regular basis. In addition, it is vital that you learn to be aware of the feelings and thoughts of your athletes just by watching them. If you are in tune with them, you will be better able to respond to them in ways that meet their needs. So, pay attention to your athletes, learn to read their body language and facial expressions, and respond to what you see. It's similar to the way the great teachers in the world can sense when their students aren't understanding a concept. Just by looking at them, the teachers know that they need to go back and re-explain the topic because some of the students are lost. The same is true of good coaches. If athletes' eyes are glazed over or the athletes appear to be disinterested in the activity, read that and respond by adjusting what you are doing to pull them back in.

Why This Matters

To be an effective coach, you must be a good teacher and a skillful communicator. Remember that one of the reasons children choose to participate in sports is to improve their skills. The extent to which they improve is partially dependent upon your ability to identify appropriate learning objectives, to design practices that will help the athletes meet those objectives, and to be capable of implementing the practice in an effective fashion. This means that you must prepare your practice sessions in advance and be able to objectively observe the session so that you can adjust as needed to achieve your learning objectives. By identifying appropriate teachable moments and then using good communication skills, you will be able to provide feedback that the athletes can use to change their behaviors and performance. The use of good communication skills will also help you maintain highly motivated athletes who are willing to listen and learn and will contribute to the development of a cohesive team that works together towards common goals.

Activity

1. Identify a piece of critical feedback that you'd like to offer one of your athletes. Write out three sentences that show how you can sandwich the criticism between a positive and a solution with encouragement.
2. Identify three activities you could do with your athletes that are completely separate from the sport but will provide an opportunity for them to get to know one another better.
3. Develop learning objectives for your next two practices. Identify activities that will help you obtain those objectives while maximizing athletes' active time.

CHAPTER FIVE

Children Are Not Miniature Adults

One of the most important things you can do as a youth coach is remember who it is that you are coaching: children. And children are not just miniature versions of adults. They do not think like adults, they do not move like adults, they do not learn like adults, and they do not judge their own success like adults. The unique characteristics of children are part of what makes coaching youth sports so much fun. However, they can also present unique challenges. Oftentimes I see coaches treating their youth athletes like adults. This might be okay if the coaches afford their youth athletes the same level of respect that they would show most adults. But, instead youth athletes are sometimes expected to behave like adults, while coaches for some reason think it is acceptable to denigrate, berate, and yell at the children. Imagine if we saw a teacher treating students the way we see many coaches treating athletes. Imagine if your supervisor at work yelled at you for a lack of effort and told you to run laps after work as a punishment. The behaviors that coaches direct at their youth athletes would not be tolerated if directed at other adults or if displayed in any setting other than sport. Be sure to treat your youth athletes as the children they are while also showing them respect as individuals. Embrace the wonderful, unique qualities of children and recognize that your coaching style should be reflective of the particular age and developmental level of the children you are coaching.

This chapter describes how children change across developmental stages. Of course, these descriptions won't be true of every child. Within any given developmental stage, the amount of variability that you might observe across individuals is likely to be large. In fact, when looking at any single individual, that individual is more likely to be above or below average than to be exactly average (Haywood and Getchell 2014). So, be sure to recognize that individual differences will be evident as you consider the developmental stages discussed and the considerations that are raised in regard to your coaching.

Another relevant point is that the recognition of self-referenced improvement is a critical contributor to an athlete's motivation to continue in a sport. So, understanding where children are developmentally is important because it will help you ensure that you are coaching your athletes to improve given their current starting point. If you ask your athletes to do things they are not yet capable of, you will be hurting their self-esteem and confidence. If you give them age-appropriate challenges, then their joy in their accomplishments will translate into a further interest in participating in the sport and a development of self-confidence that can transcend sports.

Let's now explore the various ways in which children are unique and talk about the implications for you in your coaching.

Physical Development

Physical changes are those that you are likely to see, so it might seem unnecessary to discuss them. What is important to talk about are the implications of the physical changes that children are experiencing.

DAVID AND GOLIATH

If you are coaching at the youth level, one of the things you will notice right away is that children of the same age can often come in very different sizes. This is particularly true just before and at puberty, in the age range of eleven to fourteen for boys and ten to thirteen for girls. Figure 5.1 illustrates that when working with eight-year-old girls, you may have athletes who range in size from that of a typical five-year-old to that of a typical eleven-year-old (Malina, Bourchard, and Bar-Or 2004). So, when you are coaching kids in these age ranges, it is likely that you will have some little kids, some average-sized kids, and some big kids. A few points need to be made relative to these size disparities and how they can affect your athletes.

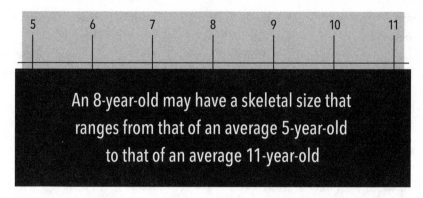

| 5 | 6 | 7 | 8 | 9 | 10 | 11 |

An 8-year-old may have a skeletal size that ranges from that of an average 5-year-old to that of an average 11-year-old

Figure 5.1. Growth rates are widely variable during adolescence, so athletes at the same chronological age can have a range of skeletal sizes.

First, as you can imagine, it can be intimidating for smaller children to play against much larger kids. This is true in all team sports, where the demands of the sport and the physical nature of the game typically give the larger child an advantage. Even if there isn't a real advantage, there is definitely an underlying influence in terms of an intimidation factor. As an example, my eleven-year-old son, James, is 4 feet, 10 inches tall and weighs 82 pounds. He is a pitcher and plays baseball against other eleven-year-olds, who range in weight from 60 to 200 pounds. On several occasions, he has faced a batter who weighs close to 200 pounds, is 5 feet, 6 inches tall, and appears to be "man-sized." When James pitches against kids this big, he is more nervous about the consequences of the hitter making contact with the ball. This then affects his willingness to throw the baseball over the plate, where the larger child can get a good hit. Of course, such a situation often results in the bigger child getting a walk, which isn't good for James's team because the fielders don't get to try to defend against a hit, nor is it good for the batter, who needs an opportunity to hit. These kinds of extreme differences in size can make an even bigger difference in collision sports such as rugby and football and contact sports such as soccer and basketball. Here, the children are regularly making physical contact with one another, and a large difference in size can affect a child's perspective of the relative safety of participating. It is perhaps not surprising that many children will tell you they have dropped out of sports because of fear of injury tied to playing against much larger children.

In youth sports, the different sizes of athletes have
implications for both the smaller kids and the larger kids.
Illustration by Dominy Alderman.

Implications

As a coach, it is important that you are sensitive to these potential concerns of your players. Think about it from their perspective. Would you
want to compete in a physical game against somebody who literally
weighs 50 percent more than you and is four inches taller? This is
what some kids are facing in their practices and games. As adults, it's
probably been a long time since we've competed against someone that
much bigger than us in size, so it's important that we consider this
from the child's perspective so that we can recognize why they might
be concerned.

If you have athletes on your team who are dramatically different
in size, such discrepancies should influence how you set up your practices. In practice situations, be sure to match children up with same-
sized children to ensure that they gain confidence by competing with
and against relatively equal-sized competitors. In other words, if you
are doing one-on-one activities, be sure to match children up by size
before getting them started. Even as you consider doing two-on-two or
small-sided games, think about making the size of the team members

relatively equal. This is a great way to get started early on in the season and will be valuable in the development of confidence. Importantly, once the children begin to have a level of confidence in their abilities, it is also beneficial to prepare smaller athletes for competition against bigger athletes. This can be done by purposefully matching up children of different sizes, by joining in the competition as an adult (albeit with constraints on the level of competitiveness you display), or by simply discussing these possibilities with the athletes in advance of competitions. It is important that children start out being confident in their abilities and then learn how to use their abilities and adapt their strategies when they face larger athletes.

· ·

KEY POINT *Big and Small Athletes on the Same Team*

- Match by size.
- Be cognizant of size advantages/disadvantages.
- Recognize risk of injury.
- Recognize that size doesn't equate to cognitive maturity.

· ·

Remember too that the difference in size also provides an advantage in noncontact sports, where being bigger typically equates to being stronger and having longer levers (that is, longer arms and legs). For example, my son Max is a fifth grader who competes for his middle school track and field team, which allows competitors from the fifth through the eighth grade. Clearly, the fifth graders are unlikely to have success (when judged as "winning"), since they are competing against athletes who are dramatically bigger and more physically mature. However, even among children who are in the same grade, the larger children have an advantage in many events. In one of their meets, five fifth-grade boys of average size threw the shot put distances ranging from 15 feet, 3 inches, to 19 feet, 1 inch. By comparison, a fifth-grade boy who is in the 95th percentile in terms of weight and height threw the shot put 26 feet, 8 inches—7 feet farther than the closest competitor! This size advantage can be seen in track and field and in many individual sports, including tennis, golf, and swimming, where longer limbs provide biomechanical advantages. Certainly the direction of the advantage is reversed in other sports like gymnastics and figure skating, where being smaller facilitates rotations and strength-to-mass ratios.

These performance advantages based on size have implications for you as the coach. The huge advantage that size can bring is but another reminder of how essential it is in youth sports to keep the focus on having fun, improving, and doing your best. When you help develop the skills of all of your athletes, irrespective of size or of their current level of ability, you can ensure that everyone has a sense of success and an interest in practicing hard and competing. Remember to work equally hard with all of your athletes and to give both smaller and bigger kids the same opportunities to compete. Sometimes youth coaches make the mistake of focusing their efforts on the bigger kids, who at that point in time are the stronger competitors. But it is critical to remember that during this stage of development, these differences in size are not necessarily predictive of athletes' ultimate size once they have matured. Nor is their current level of performance predictive of what they might ultimately achieve. Furthermore, remember that our goal isn't to identify and develop only the best athletes; rather, our goal is to help *all* athletes improve so that they can all continue to have personal satisfaction from their efforts in sports.

··

KEY POINT *Judging Ability*

Do not make judgments about the ability of young athletes based solely on their physical size.

··

Another consideration that I have to mention concerns the perspective of the larger kid. Although certainly bigger kids can be very skillful, athletic, and adroit, it is also common that they have experienced recent growth spurts and may not have full control of their bodily movements. I have seen parents and officials react differently to bigger children than they do to smaller children, particularly when there is physical contact between children of different sizes. If a larger kid and a smaller kid collide, the larger kid may attract most of the "blame" for the collision and may receive negative feedback from the other team, the other team's coaches and fans, and even the official. If you have bigger kids on your team, you may want to discuss such concerns with them so that they are mentally prepared for experiencing sports as a larger child.

A final point relative to these size discrepancies: size does not equate to cognitive, emotional, or social maturity. It is easy for adults to make the mistake of assuming higher levels of maturity in bigger kids. Expectations for these kids may then be inappropriate in terms of their potential to act as leaders, to manage their emotions, and to cognitively process abstract concepts. Similarly, smaller kids are not necessarily less mature than the bigger kids. In fact, physical size and maturity are independent of one another, and it is essential that you gauge an individual child's abilities rather than make assumptions based upon size. Be sure to respond to each child relative to his or her own level of maturity and offer kids challenges in sports that meet them where they are.

PUBERTY

There are two major points that are important to bear in mind with respect to coaching youth athletes who have not reached puberty. First, many coaches do not realize that before puberty, endurance training does not have a very big impact on aerobic fitness. Aerobic fitness in children is largely determined by chronological age, and changes in aerobic fitness over time are largely due to growth and maturation (Armstrong, Tomkinson, and Ekelund 2011), which all act independently and which can affect fitness in the absence of an endurance training program. In fact, evidence suggests that endurance training programs result in only a 5–6 percent gain in fitness for children who are prepubescent (Baquet, van Praagh, and Berthoin 2003; Payne et al. 1997; Rowland 2005). And note that this is the typical response to a *program of endurance training*. The point here is that unless you are coaching endurance sports like track, cross-country, or swimming, the time you have with your athletes for practice is better spent on keeping them actively engaged in sport-related activity than having them run exclusively. So, for example, rather than have your football team run laps, ask them to play a moving toss and catch game with the football. This can be done in a delineated space where some of the kids have a football and some do not and they simply run in the space with the restriction that they must toss the ball within five steps after they have caught the ball. This kind of activity has an aerobic component but also includes game-related skills that will transfer to the sport, and it is certainly more fun than running laps around the field. Prior to puberty, the focus on technical and tactical aspects of the sport is more critical than a focus on fitness training.

Second, it is important to recognize that children in this age range are likely to be experiencing rapid growth. The growth spurt for a boy typically occurs between ten and eighteen years of age and may reach a peak growth rate of eight to twelve centimeters a year (Hawkins and Metheny 2001). Think about the impact of a growth spurt on a child's center of balance and ability to control his or her limbs. Children who have experienced a growth spurt have changes in their gait patterns that may influence their ability to perform in sports (Bisi and Stagni 2016). In addition, overuse injuries are more common in children during their growth spurts. This is because limbs may grow by as much as four centimeters during a growth spurt, with muscles and tendons lengthening without concomitant increases in muscle mass. As a result, to generate the same amount of force as was previously generated, the muscle must now work at a higher percentage of its maximum capability. This puts a strain on the muscles and on the elongated tendons. As their coach, it is important for you to be sensitive to the changes that your athletes experience in response to a growth spurt and to recognize the implications. You may, for example, have an athlete who was among the most skillful the previous year but is having difficulty achieving the same level of performance during a year of rapid growth. If this is the case, you should express empathy and understanding and be supportive of the athlete's efforts to improve with his or her "new body." In addition, recognize that because the growth spurt is a result of rapidly growing limbs, muscles and tendons may be at risk for injury. Furthermore, frustration about an inability to perform as well as they could previously may lead to athletes exerting additional effort to regain previous performance levels. As a result, these young athletes may put themselves at an increased risk of overtraining and overuse injuries.

AGE-APPROPRIATE CHALLENGES

One last consideration is to be sure that the game is adjusted to provide the athletes with the appropriate challenge. For instance, in youth basketball, the goal height and ball size are adjusted relative to age (Kendall 2018). In youth soccer, the numbers of players on each team and the ball and goal size are different for the different age groups. In youth tennis, the rackets and courts are smaller and balls that have reduced bounce are used for younger athletes to ensure early success. And in baseball and softball, the entire field is sized differently for the different age groups. So, if you are coaching at the younger ages, be sure that you advise the athletes to purchase appropriately sized balls and equipment and follow age-appropriate guidelines for your sport to allow them the opportunity to be successful at their current age and size.

....

KEY POINT *Before Puberty Sets In*

- Girls and boys can compete together.
- Aerobic and strength training provide only small benefits.
- Rapid growth can result in a lack of coordination.
- Rapid growth can lead to greater risk of injury.

....

Motor Skill Development

Although there is great variability in physical growth among children, there is arguably even more variability in motor skill development. This is because motor skill development is influenced by so many factors, including age, height, weight, biological sex, environment, and experience. There are, however, some identifiable motor development stages that children move through and that are generally evident at particular age ranges.

WALKING, TALKING, *OR* CHEWING GUM

Children between two and seven years of age are in a phase of motor development called the fundamental movement phase. I have informally named this stage the walking, talking, *or* chewing gum stage because at these ages children can truly do only one of these activities at a time. During this phase, children are just beginning to gain control over both gross and fine motor skills. Gross motor skills require the use of large muscles of the body and include stability skills such as bending and stretching; locomotor skills like running, jumping, and skipping; and manipulative skills like bouncing, kicking, or catching a ball (Gallahue and Ozmun 2006). From two to seven years of age, most children move from initial efforts to perform the skill, to elementary proficiency at the skill, to a mature stage of skill performance.

Initial efforts are literally the first attempts to perform these various gross motor skills. So, for walking, we know that most infants take their very first steps between nine and twelve months of age and that they begin to walk well when they are fourteen to fifteen months old. At these ages, one of the best activities for them to be engaged in is simply playing at a park. Here they have the opportunity to run, climb, balance, swing, and navigate obstacles. These fundamental movement skills provide them with the necessary foundations to further refine their skills as they get older. But, remember that some youth sports organizations are offering to enroll children into their sports programs as early as eighteen months! This is only three to four months after they have just learned to walk well! Clearly, for these children, there is no need for programming to be sport-specific as they are simply trying to learn how to do these most basic of movements. At this age, the organized sports offerings are typically focused on kids participating with their parents. So, the coach is actually more of a facilitator whose responsibility is to engage the parents and the kids in fun activities.

As children reach an elementary level of proficiency, they begin to look slightly more coordinated in their movements. Four-year-olds can walk alongside their parents with ease and can run to get places. But if you've been around four-year-olds much, you know that this is a time of boo-boos and Band-Aids because it doesn't take much in terms of an environmental challenge for them to lose their balance, trip, and fall. During this age, there is clearly still no reason to be sport-specific, as children have not yet mastered these most fundamental of movements. At this age, activities might begin to incorporate aspects of a sport, but the activities themselves should still be focused exclusively on fun.

As children turn five to six years of age, most reach the mature stage, which is a time when their fundamental movements appear to be much more coordinated and resistant to small challenges. Reaching this stage is critical because it is foundational for the learning of sports skills, which require them to combine fundamental movements. When working with children in this age group, coaches can begin to focus on fundamental movement skills that are important for their sport. For example, they might use games that focus on running and changing direction, on throwing at targets at variable distances, or on dribbling a ball with either hand. Coaches should recognize that most elementary-age children and many adolescents have not mastered these fundamental movement skills (Hardy et al. 2012), which are a prerequisite to achieving higher levels of proficiency within a sport. Hence, it is important that you take the time with your athletes to help them develop these skills.

Implications

As a coach, if you are working with these younger children, knowledge of where they are developmentally can help you be more effective. In the first place, recognize that children between two and seven years old are literally not yet capable of combining fundamental movements. So, it is not the time to expect children to be able to perform tasks like striking a moving ball while on the run, standing on one leg while kicking, or running and catching at the same time. Rather, it is important for you to be patient with these youngsters and to keep your focus on helping them develop their fundamental movement skills to a mature level while having fun in the sport. Fundamental movement skills will progress to an elementary proficiency level on their own, but to advance to a mature level requires practice, encouragement, and age-appropriate challenges. As the coach of young children in any sport, keep your focus on fundamental movement skills so that you prepare your athletes for more sport-specific skills in the future.

Design your practices to incorporate a lot of activities that engage these skills. For example, play a game of Simon Says, where you encourage the athletes to pay attention to the leader, who instructs them to run in place, jump up, jump back, jump to the side, skip, hop, stand and throw a ball to themselves and catch it, or bounce a ball and catch it. You can play a game of freeze tag, where you can get "unfrozen" if you execute some required movement (like jump up and down five times). You can play a game that my kids invented (and that I loved!) called kick-and-catch. When we first played, they were four and six years of age. At that time, I would lightly kick (punt) a kickball up in the air so that one of the children could try to catch it. I would kick it gently and right to them so that they didn't have to move much to make the catch. After getting control of the ball, that child would then get it back to me either by kicking it, throwing it, or running it back to me. As they got older and better at the game, I would kick the ball a little higher or kick the ball so that they had to move a little to catch it. Think about all the fundamental movement skills that were incorporated into this game. The children had to watch the ball, judge its distance, move to intercept, catch the ball (or pursue it after a drop), and then get the ball to the kicker. Importantly, this was an easy game to adjust relative to the skill level of the particular child so that the challenge level was appropriate and individualized. I encourage you to be creative and to consult available resources to identify activities and games you can use to help your athletes practice and develop their fundamental movement skills. Your work with them at this age will be critical to mastering these movements, which will allow them to progress to more sport-specific types of activities.

· ·

KEY POINT *Fundamental Movement Skills*

The mastery of fundamental movement skills is critical to the performance of sports skills.

· ·

WALKING, TALKING, *AND* CHEWING GUM

At its broad level, this phase takes our athletes from seven years of age through adulthood. In this phase, individuals can now combine the performance of their motor skills, making sports performance much more enjoyable. This phase can be further broken down into a transitional phase, an application phase, and a lifelong utilization phase.

The transitional phase takes place from age seven to ten years. During this phase, athletes begin combining fundamental skills to perform specialized sports skills. So, you can now ask athletes to perform a locomotor skill in combination with a manipulative skill. For example, you can ask them to run *while* dribbling a soccer ball or a basketball, to hit a tennis ball *while* on the move, or to use their legs to develop power *while* executing a volleyball pass. This is a period where huge gains in performance can be achieved by your young athletes. However, the activities that they can do will be reliant upon them having already mastered the underlying fundamental skills. In other words, your ability to help your athletes advance is going to be dependent upon them bringing those fundamental skills with them to your practice. If the fundamental movement skills are not fully developed, you would be wise to spend time honing those before moving on to more complex activities.

When you first meet with your athletes, it's a great opportunity to observe them performing fundamental skills to get a sense of their level of mastery. If your athletes are able to run efficiently, to balance on one leg, to hop, to skip, and to gallop, then they may have mastery of the locomotion skills. If they can throw and catch or strike a ball with an implement, then they have some mastery of their manipulative skills. And if they can stand on one leg, jump onto a target, and maintain their balance, they have mastery over their stabilizing skills. Activities that you can design for your athletes now will help them learn to skillfully combine fundamental movement skills. With this age group, games of sharks and minnows will allow athletes to demonstrate their ability to move while dribbling. Sharks and minnows is a game that many children play in the swimming pool, but it can be adapted to team sports like soccer, field hockey, and basketball. In these sports, you would set up a grid with all the children with a ball at one end of the grid (these are the "minnows") and one player without a ball who is in the middle of the grid (the "shark"). When the coach says "go," the minnows try to dribble their balls to the far side of the grid without the shark stealing a ball from them. Anyone who loses the ball becomes a shark for the next round. You keep playing until all of the minnows have been caught. One great aspect of this game is that kids aren't knocked out—everyone gets to play the entire time! Games of tag while handling a ball are also possible for warm-up activities. And activities where you begin to work on accuracy of a pass during gamelike activities will be manageable.

With my kids, we further adapted the kick-and-catch game to provide an appropriate challenge for them at this age. The first modification we made was that I would punt the ball at different heights, requiring them to move varying distances to be able to make the catch. I made up a point system so that catching a more difficult ball was worth more points than a less difficult ball. And if the ball bounced first, they could get half of the points. This game was very motivating to the kids and taught them to combine skills of running and catching, gave them experience judging the path of flighted balls, and (as a side note) allowed us to practice some math skills. Again, once they caught it, they returned it to me however they wanted to.

Think carefully about using "knock-out" games. When these are played, those who are eliminated are typically the weakest players on the team. So, if they're knocked out early, how are they going to benefit from the activity? If you must use a knock-out game, then be sure to figure out ways for the athletes who are removed to get back into the game. For example, maybe they do a sport skill five times or do ten jumping jacks to get back into the activity. There doesn't have to be a winner. If it's a game that is going to help the athletes develop their skills, just keep it going by letting athletes back into the game.

The next modification was that now the kids were the ones kicking. Each would try to punt the ball toward the other kids, who were facing the kicker (and somewhat distributed across the space). In this modification, the rule was that they could kick until someone else caught the ball or ten times, whichever came first. This was great as well because now they were learning to punt a ball, to control the direction of the punt, and to control the distance and height of the punt. The catchers were still learning how to judge flighted balls and to catch while on the run. From a life-skills perspective, they were also having to think about issues of sportsmanship, fairness, and competitiveness. This game was such a favorite for my kids that they took it to their elementary school and have many fond memories of playing kick-and-catch with their friends in third and fourth grade.

The next phase of motor development within this broad age range is the application phase, which occurs from ages eleven to fourteen. This is a critically important time period in part because this is when many athletes start to make decisions about which sports they want to pursue into adolescence. It is also at this time that young athletes begin to see sports as a part of their identity and to start to describe themselves as softball players or tennis players or gymnasts. During this phase, sports begin to be played in a way that more closely resembles the way it is played by adults. Gone are the days of Pac-Man soccer, playing it over on the first pass in volleyball, and no-hit baseball; welcome to the days of combination passing, pass-set-hit, and double plays. This makes spectating and coaching much more enjoyable as the improvements in skill are so evident. This higher level of play is not just because of the development of motor skills but also because of cognitive developments that allow players to understand their sport at a higher level. This is a time when, as a coach, it is really important to focus on the "perfect" execution of skills because it is during this phase that perfect practice will lead to an automaticity of the skill that will allow it to be displayed properly in stressful gamelike situations. It is also an incredibly rewarding time to coach because of the huge gains in performance that are possible with this age group. Athletes' bodies are physically and cognitively ready to take advantage of practice opportunities, competitive events, and constructive feedback to hone their sports skills.

The final phase of motor development is called the lifelong utilization phase. It is in this stage that athletes in many sports begin to approach their peak performance levels. In fact, some athletes even start to compete against adults as early as fourteen years of age. Think about Jennifer Capriati, who made it to the finals of a professional tennis tournament just before she turned fourteen. Or consider Freddy Adu, who signed a professional contract in Major League Soccer and played in a professional game when he was only fourteen. Although these players are clearly rare prodigies, they provide an illustration of what is possible during this age range. So, if you have the opportunity to coach young athletes in this age range and if they have been given the appropriate training previously, it is possible to help them make big gains in terms of their technical skills, tactical choices, and performance. It is during these years that you can help them not only to continue to develop as athletes but also to maintain a love for the game through the use of positive coaching techniques.

Cognitive Development

Another important type of development to consider is cognitive development. This essentially refers to a child's abilities to comprehend and make judgments about the world around him or her. According to psychologist Jean Piaget's theory of cognitive developmental stages (1971), young people move through the concrete operational stage from five to nine years of age and then enter the formal operational stage at ten to eleven years.

During the concrete operational stage, children's thinking is tied closely to concrete objects. In ball sports, that concrete object is only one thing: the ball! When you coach children in this age range, it is critical to remember that the only thing they will see as important is the ball. So, if there is only one ball, then every child on the team will be chasing that one ball. Thus, as a coach, you would be wise to ask every child on your team to bring a ball to practice. That way, you can ensure that every child has constant access to the one thing they care about at this age. And why not? Remember, it is during this age range that you are trying to help the children move from the fundamental movement phase to the specialized movement phase. So, make sure every child has a ball, and when they're in the fundamental movement phase, have them do lots of activities where they are interacting with the ball.

During this phase, you should be trying to get the kids as many "touches on the ball" as possible. It amazes me how often I will see coaches running a practice with ten or more young children standing in a line waiting for their one opportunity to interact with the ball. What this means is that at any given time, there is only one child with a ball and there are nine or more without. How can that possibly be any fun for the nine who are waiting in line? Remember, in this age range, they can focus only on concrete objects, and the one reason they came to play is because they want to play with the ball. So, incorporate one ball per person into all of your activities so that you maximize their opportunity to develop motor skills for your sport. If you are coaching a sport that is not a ball sport, this conversation is still relevant. You won't have to think hard to identify what it is that they are interested in. It may be the tumbling mat, the swimming pool, or the track. They definitely do not want to watch others perform or to listen to a coach talk! So, again, remember why they are there and what makes it fun and get them to it as quickly as possible (while obviously maintaining any necessary safety considerations).

Another thing to consider with children in this age range is that they are not ready for many sport-related concepts that you might want to share with them. For instance, they will not be able to understand what you mean when you ask them to stretch the defense. They won't comprehend what it means for a team to have a "shape." They won't understand yet how "man on" should influence their decision-making.

They won't see the link between a quick start time and the total time of a race. Although it is fine to begin introducing these concepts, it is important that you do not get frustrated when they are not fully able to grasp your instructions. Instead, introduce the concepts while also getting them lots of repetitions of the motor movements incorporating the requisite skill sets.

TIME, DISTANCE, AND PACE

After the concrete operational stage, ten- to eleven-year-olds begin to move into a stage where they can engage in abstract thought processes. This is when children start to understand the multiple causal variables that determine an outcome. So, for the first time, they will begin to recognize that a pass to a teammate should be accurate and should be delivered at the correct pace to allow their teammate to receive the pass. They will start to see that when they move without the ball, the passing lanes change for the person with the ball. Coupled with their progression into the specialized movement phase, these cognitive gains make coaching at this age an incredibly rewarding experience. This is when you can begin to combine technical training with tactical training so that huge gains in individual and team performance can be observed. For athletes in this stage, it is a critical window when you can help them make big gains as athletes while still ensuring that they have fun playing and get satisfaction from their improvements.

Psychosocial Development

The last form of development for us to talk about is psychosocial development, where I am referring to how children view themselves and to what extent they care about the opinions of others. In many ways, this is one of the harder aspects of development for us to recognize because while it is all happening in the minds of the children, it can have a big impact on how they approach sports.

"I AM GOOD AT EVERYTHING"

The five- to nine-year-old range is really a beautiful time in terms of psychosocial development. These children tend to have a positive sense of self-worth that is based on a concrete and positive view of reality. The youngest children in this age range have an "I can do it" attitude that is refreshing. As an adult, have you ever been asked by a five-year-old to have a footrace? Chances are, that child fully believes that he or she can beat you in the race. And, since many adults choose to allow the five-year-old to win (either easily or by a nose), that belief is often reinforced. But what if you choose to beat the five-year-old? That is where you will see something really cool! The child will ask you to race again. You might wonder why, since you are clearly the better runner. The reason is because the five-year-old really believes he or she can beat you! Five-year-olds are not limited by judgments of physical capabilities, stride length, experience, or age. Nope. Five-year-olds believe they can do anything they set their minds to, and they believe the fun is in the doing.

So, with this younger age group, your responsibility is to help them maintain that "I can do it" attitude for as long as possible. Encourage them to always try their hardest. Reinforce their efforts. Reward them with positive comments when you see them try something new (whether it's successful or not). When working with children this age, it is important that you get them to give their best effort in everything they do and to reward them for giving that effort. This doesn't mean that you ask them to sprint all the time in an activity or that you focus on fitness or work rate. What it means is that you reinforce the effort they are giving so that you will see increasingly more effort. Think about it this way. Imagine you are coaching a team of eight-year-olds and you do the following:

1. Through your activities, you give them the opportunity for repeated exposure to the sports skills they need.
2. Through your reinforcement of effort, you get the kids to consistently give a high level of effort.
3. Through trying something new, you get kids to be willing to stretch their comfort zones.

What do you think will happen? If you do this consistently with your athletes, what will happen is that you will end up with athletes who improve their skills, consistently give high effort, and are unafraid to try something new. What better situation could you ask for as a coach? If you have a group of athletes who are doing this, then you have a group of athletes who will improve at the sport while also enjoying their participation and gaining satisfaction from their own personal growth.

KEY POINT *The Importance of Trying*

Remind your athletes that trying means working hard, concentrating on what they are doing, giving their best effort, and being willing to perform new skills. If they stop trying, they will never win. But if they keep trying, they have the chance to win today and they increase their chances of winning tomorrow.

"AM I GOOD AT ANYTHING?"

When kids are in the age range of ten to eleven years old (fourth and fifth grade), they enter a stage where social comparison becomes more important. It is at this age that many children start having a strong opinion about things like the brand name of their sneakers and the style of their clothes. This is because they are now starting to notice and care about what other people are doing and wearing. As a funny example, when he was ten one of my sons decided to start using Dapper Dan (hair gel) to get his hair to look a certain way. He'd never cared about his hair before, but all of a sudden his looks mattered to him. The challenging part about this period is that at the same time that they are starting to care what other people think about them, they are also beginning to have their own positive and negative self-evaluations. In other words, they are starting to be able to differentiate effort and ability so that they no longer think that trying hard necessarily makes you the winner. They now recognize that children have different levels of ability and that no matter how hard they try, they might not be able to outperform another athlete. What is fascinating during this time period, however, is that effort and ability are not yet fully differentiated. In other words, kids in this age range still want to believe that effort can make a difference even in the face of differences in ability. So, right now, my twin boys are eleven years old, and Max is faster than James. James will regularly ask me if I think that he could be faster than Max if he were to train harder. James runs all the time at recess and at PE and is committed to running track and cross-country. I don't know if James will ever be faster than Max, no matter how hard he tries. But, what I do know is that if James quits trying, he will definitely never be faster. If he keeps at it and trains hard and gives it his best, then maybe one day he will be faster, and even if he isn't, he can be satisfied that he gave it his all.

··

KEY QUESTION *What Should You Focus On: Process or Outcome?*

- If you focus on the process, you can obtain an outcome.
- If you focus on an outcome, you can increase your commitment to the process.
- If you are apathetic about the process, you will never obtain the outcome.
- If you are apathetic about the outcome, you will have a hard time staying committed to the process.

You must stay focused on both process and outcome to be successful!

··

THE DIFFERENTIATION OF LUCK, EFFORT, AND ABILITY

Let me tell you about an experiment testing whether children could fully distinguish between luck and effort (Fry 2000) (see fig. 5.2). Young children (five- to six-year-olds), children (seven- to eleven-year-olds), and preadolescents (twelve- to thirteen-year-olds) were asked to throw a beanbag into one of four colored baskets. In the first condition, they drew a card indicating the color of basket to aim for and then threw the bag. In the second condition, they were asked to throw the bag into a basket and then to draw a card indicating which color was the right basket to have thrown it into. As you read and think about this, I'm sure it's clear that the first condition is a skill condition and the second is a luck condition. But, when the children were asked if there was any difference between the conditions, the answers differed by age group. The young children said that they could do better if they tried harder in both conditions. The next older group of children recognized that the second condition was harder, but they still believed that they could do better if they tried harder. The preadolescents recognized that trying harder would help in the first condition but would not make a difference in the second.

	AGE GROUP		
	5–6 yrs	7–11 yrs	12–13 yrs
First condition (Skill) 1. Choose card to find color 2. Throw bean bag into matching basket	I could do better if I tried harder	Luck game is harder, but I could do better if I try harder	Trying harder will improve outcome
Second condition (Luck) 1. Throw bean bag into basket of your choice 2. Choose card to see if you picked the right basket			Trying harder will not improve outcome

Figure 5.2. An interesting study used a bean-bag-tossing task to demonstrate that children's ability to differentiate between effort and luck changes as they age.

Do you see why these examples are so important? If you are working with children who are younger than twelve years of age, it is critical that you help them to focus on effort and not on ability. At this age, there is no limit to what they can accomplish. So, don't put limits on them. Help them to value their hard work, to demonstrate persistence, to put in the effort, and to appreciate what they put into their sport more than what they get out of it. If you can help your athletes focus on the process rather than on the outcome, you have the potential to help them maintain joy in their sport regardless of outcome. And if they maintain their joy for the sport and keep trying, you just never know what might happen in terms of sports success.

Once children reach twelve years of age, they can now fully differentiate ability, luck, and effort. Think about this time period. This is the end of sixth grade or the start of seventh grade. Middle school. Do you remember middle school? For many people, middle school was one of the toughest periods of their lives. And understanding what happens psychosocially during middle school probably helps to explain this phenomenon. During middle school, children start to perceive more critical evaluation from others, which can lead them to self-criticize. They now start to describe themselves as being good at certain things and bad at other things. For example, in sports they might say they are a really good forward but not a good defensive player. Or they might say that they are good at shooting but not good at passing. They will begin to pigeonhole themselves in ways that restrict their ability to try new things and to be willing to risk failure. This is a time when it is important to help them further develop both a process and an outcome orientation (see chapter 9). The middle school years can be a difficult time for young athletes, but it is one when a coach who is caring, empathetic, and focused on process before outcome can help these athletes maintain their willingness to work hard in their sport.

....

Table 5.1. Developmental readiness relative to chronological age

Ages	Motor skills development
2–7	Can do only fundamental movement skills.
7–10	Can combine fundamental movement skills.
11–14	Can refine more complex skills through practice.
14+	Performance can look experienced.

Ages	Cognitive development
5–9	Concrete stage. Can focus on only one thing (the most important object).
10–11+	Abstract stage. Can make more advanced judgments about how variables work together.

Ages	Social development
5–9	I am good at everything. Trying hard = being good at something.
10–11	What other people think about me matters and I'm unsure of my abilities.

Ages	Capacity to distinguish between ability and effort
5–6	Can't distinguish. Trying hard = high ability.
7–11	Can partially distinguish. Ability matters but believe trying hard is most important.
12+	Can fully distinguish. Trying hard matters, but it definitely can't overcome ability.

....

Why This Matters

Coaches have the opportunity to spend a lot of time working with their athletes. It is important that coaches remember that children are not miniature adults and that the athletes in each age group will be at a particular stage in their development. To be a good coach, you must meet the children where they are in terms of their developmental readiness.

When you design your practices, keep in mind where the children are in terms of their physical, motor skill, cognitive, and psychosocial development. Keep the practices active and fun and focus on the skill sets that make sense based on their age. Be empathetic and sensitive to their growth as young people, and help your athletes concentrate on their own personal improvement to ensure that they can self-reference and find satisfaction in every practice and competition.

Activity

Identify the age group you are coaching. Look at table 5.1 to help you identify where your athletes are in terms of their developmental readiness. Describe your athletes below.

PHYSICAL
_____

_____

COGNITIVE
_____

_____

MOTOR
_____

_____

PSYCHOSOCIAL
_____

_____

Now, consider the implications for your practices. What are some key elements of your practices that should reflect where these athletes are relative to all of these aspects?

_____

_____

_____

_____

_____

CHAPTER SIX

Blue and Pink

Gender Bias in Society

One of the topics that is frequently brought up at coaching clinics is whether girls and boys should be coached differently This question is driven by the almost constant barrage of images, anecdotes, and individual experiences that reinforce the notion that there are big differences between girls and boys. But you might be surprised to learn what the evidence shows.

We live in a gendered world, and the experience of girls and boys is not exactly the same. In fact, gender-based treatment starts even before birth. When families find out that they are expecting a baby, many rush to create the perfect environment in which to bring their newborn. If the baby is a girl, then the nursery is typically decked out in shades of pink and purple with plenty of lace and frill. If the baby is a boy, then the nursery is more often painted in shades of blue with more practical accessories. Many parents may try to be more gender-neutral in their nursery decor, but that is only the first battle they have to fight to avoid societal and cultural influences.

The impact of societal norms on children continues through childhood and comes from multiple sources. These norms are reinforced through interactions with adults, through the media, and through advertising. For example, boys are encouraged to be more "rough and tumble," while girls are rewarded for being more nurturing and demure. When a boy falls and hurts himself, adults will often encourage him to jump up and shake it off. By contrast, when a girl falls and hurts herself, adults rush to her side to make sure she is okay. We see it in the media as well. If you have a flyer or a magazine for a toy store available in your home (you probably have several if the winter holidays are near!), take a look at the pictures that include boys and those that include girls. If you don't have one of these handy, check out an online toy store like Hearth Song or Fat Brain Toys and compare the science and arts and crafts sections. Typically, when you find pictures of girls, you'll see them playing with toys like a cash register, a doll with hair you can actually style, or a cooking set. By contrast, you'll see boys using a telescope, playing with trucks, or painting a wooden birdhouse. Of course, over time advertising has become somewhat more gender-neutral, but societal norms displayed through advertising persist today. These differences reinforce gender-based stereotypes of appropriate activities and career paths for boys and girls and are reflected in all facets of society.

Sports are no exception to this pattern of gender-based stereotypes. For instance, we know that girls begin to play organized sports on average six months later than boys (Sabo and Veliz 2011). Furthermore, fathers are more likely to spend time playing sports with their sons than with their daughters (Sabo and Veliz 2011). Also, although there are relatively equal numbers of girls and boys participating in at least one organized sport per year, boys are more likely to play multiple sports and have more opportunities to play high school sports than girls (Sabo and Veliz 2011). So, in terms of access to sports, there are clearly gender-related differences. And these may be reflected in terms of the athletic ability displayed by girls compared with that of boys. Boy or girl, if you haven't had as much exposure to an activity, you won't be able to perform that activity as skillfully, and this may limit your interest in sports.

....

KEY POINT *The Insult*

There is nothing I hate to hear more than "You throw like a girl." Have you ever seen an elite-level female softball player throw a ball? There is nothing "girl-like" about it. When a skillful girl throws a ball, she does not look any different than a skillful boy. So, a more appropriate criticism for someone's poor throwing would be "You throw like a novice."

....

Gender differences in participation are also evident through the ranks of coaches. The sex distribution of youth sports coaches is very lopsided, with about 73 percent male coaches and only about 27 percent female coaches (Flanagan 2017). Thus, most female youth athletes and almost all male youth athletes will have been coached by men during their sports careers. I am frequently asked by male coaches, "What do I need to do differently when I coach girls, compared with when I coach boys?" This seems a logical question, given all the gender-based differences between boys and girls that are reinforced in society. But the real question is, *are* there differences between boys and girls that should affect the way that they are coached in sports?

. . . .

KEY POINT *Who Are the Coaches?*

During their athletic careers, almost all boys and the majority of girls will be coached exclusively by men. Female coaches almost never have the opportunity to coach boys.

. . . .

Evidence of Perceived Gender Differences

Let's consider this question of whether or not differences between boys and girls should influence how we coach by taking a look at popular coaching books available online. The answer according to these resources appears to be "yes." Looking at published books on coaching, you will see plenty of evidence suggesting that there is much you need to know about coaching girls but that coaching boys does not require any unique skill sets. Try it out yourself. Go to a search engine for an online bookstore and look for "coaching girls." I did this within the books category on Amazon in May 2018 and got 585 results. Many of the books had titles suggesting that they had important information to offer relative to coaching girls in a broad range of sports (for example, *How to Coach Girls* and *Was it Something I Said? A Guide to Coaching Female Athletes*). There were also sport-specific books for almost every sport imaginable with titles reinforcing this notion that there are specific things you need to know if you are going to coach girls (such as *Coaching Girls' Soccer* and *Coaching Girls' Softball*).

KEY POINT *The Large Number of Books
Focused on Coaching Girls**

DeWitt, J. 2001. *Coaching Girls' Soccer*. New York: Three Rivers Press.

Dicicco, T., and C. Hacker. 2002. *Catch Them Being Good: Everything You Need to Know to Successfully Coach Girls*. New York: Viking Penguin.

Hatchell, S. 2006. *The Complete Guide to Coaching Girls' Basketball: Building a Great Team the Carolina Way*. Camden, Me.: McGraw-Hill.

LaPrath, D. 2009. *Coaching Girls' Soccer Successfully*. Champaign, Ill.: Human Kinetics.

Potash, W. J. 2012. *They're Not Boys: Safely Training the Adolescent Female Athlete*. Learn2trainsafely.com.

Simpson, S. 2001. *Coaching Girls' Basketball: From the How-To's of the Game to Practical Real-World Advice—Your Definitive Guide to Successfully Coaching Girls*. New York: Three Rivers Press.

Strahan, K. 2001. *Coaching Girls' Softball*. Roseville, Calif.: Prima Publishing.

Tucker, J. 2003. *Coaching Girls' Lacrosse: A Baffled Parent's Guide*. Camden, Me.: Ragged Mountain Press.

*Sample from the first 50 featured hits on Amazon.com.

When I searched for "coaching boys," I still got a lot of hits (400), but the titles were very different in that they weren't really focused on the coaching of boys at all. In fact, I did not find any books that discussed coaching boys across sports, and I had to scroll through three pages of search results to find a paltry three books with titles suggesting they were focused on boy-specific coaching for a particular sport.

KEY POINT *The Much Smaller Number of Books
Focused on Coaching Boys (This Is All of Them!)*

Murrell, G. P., and J. Garland. 2002. *Coaching Boys' Lacrosse*. Camden, Me.: Ragged Mountain Press.

Mylott, T. 2009. *Kids' Lacrosse: A Guide to Coaching Elementary School Boys' Lacrosse*. CreateSpace Independent Publishing Platform.

Van Huis, J. 2009. *Coaching the Little Boys of Summer: Fathers, Sons, and the Experience of Youth Baseball*. Holland, Mich.: Black Lake Press.

So, what does this huge difference in the number of popular-press books focused on coaching girls as compared with coaching boys suggest? It implies that there is much we need to know about coaching girls that is specific to them and that is not generic to the game.

I want to emphasize that popular-press books aren't *evidence* that there are actual differences between the sexes that are relevant to coaching. Rather, I share this with you because I want to make a point. The point is that the societal biases that influence how we interact with boys and girls are reinforced through some of the popular coaching resources that are available. The sheer volume of coaching books focused on girls reinforce "pink and blue" stereotypes. Scientists have also discovered that topics discussed in books on coaching girls differ from those discussed in books on coaching boys (see Scientific Evidence: Comparison of Coaching Topics for Girls and Those for Boys below). However, these stereotypical ideas are typically *not* supported by any scientific evidence of actual differences between boys and girls that should impact your coaching. In fact, the existing evidence tells us exactly the opposite—*effective coaching techniques will be effective regardless of the sex of the athletes.*

....

SCIENTIFIC EVIDENCE *Comparison of Coaching Topics for Girls and Boys*

When popular coaching books were analyzed by scientists (LaVoi, Becker, and Maxwell 2007), those focused on coaching girls suggested that

- there are *problems* with coaching girls,
- coaching boys is normative while coaching girls is different, and
- young female athletes have characteristics that will make them more challenging to coach than boys.

....

Evidence of Actual Gender Differences

So, let's now switch our focus to what we actually know about differences between boys and girls that might have real implications for how you should coach your team. In fact, despite the proliferation of popular books, *there is actually very little scientific research that has been conducted to explore differences between boys and girls* or between men and women that might affect how you should treat your athletes. And, *much of this research actually speaks to similarities between the sexes as much as it speaks to differences.*

COGNITION, PERSONALITY, AND BEHAVIORS

Researchers have explored differences as a function of gender in everything from gregariousness to mathematical skills. Much of this comes from work done with adults, but there is also some limited evidence from studies that have compared boys and girls. When these studies are summarized, we find that girls and boys are similar in more ways than they are different. In fact, some of the ways that they are similar argue strongly against gender-based stereotypes.

For example, you've likely heard it said that girls' verbal skills are naturally better than boys' and that boys' math skills are naturally better than girls'. As it turns out, standardized test performance shows us that the difference between boys and girls in verbal skills is small, (Hyde 2014) and, based upon data from 7 million students in grades 2–11, the differences in their mathematics performance is trivial (Hyde et al. 2008). So, there's one gender stereotype out the window! Girls and boys are also similar in how they view themselves and their skills. This is clearly relevant to coaching because it is important for you to recognize that while most children (and adults) will experience times when they doubt their ability and feel uncertain, these doubts are not gender-based. Therefore, you should expect to see similar fluctuations in confidence in boys and girls, and you should manage the situation in the same way for boys and girls by helping all athletes recognize their strengths and accomplishments. In terms of emotions, girls are stereotypically viewed as being more emotional and less able to experience pride than boys. However, research indicates that this is not the case (Hyde 2014). In other words, again, boys and girls are the same in terms of their ability to express both positive and negative emotions.

Therefore, we should expect boys and girls to respond similarly to their performance and the outcome of competition.

In terms of aggression, we see both similarities and differences between boys and girls. When talking about aggression here, it is important to point out that the evidence in this area is specific to negative forms of aggression, which are behaviors intended to cause physical or psychological harm. The evidence indicates that boys and girls display similar amounts of nonphysical aggression (for example, attacking others verbally or attempting to damage others' relationships with their peers). This runs counter to the recent stereotypes of "mean girls," which incorrectly suggest that girls are more prone to display nonphysical negative aggression than boys. The implication is that if you are coaching boys, you should not be lulled into a false sense of security with respect to the potential for this form of aggression. Both boys and girls may display nonphysical negative aggression toward teammates or opponents.

In contrast, with physical forms of negative aggression there *are* observable differences between boys and girls. In fact, these differences appear as early as the age of two, with boys being more likely to be more physically aggressive than girls (Baillargeon et al. 2007), and these differences are evident at all ages and across cultures (Archer 2004). This has implications for you as a coach in that if you are coaching boys, you may need to be prepared to cope with aggressive behavior displayed in competition. For instance, what will you do if you have an athlete who displays aggression that results in penalties? It will be important for you to address this with the athlete so that he understands the difference between physical play that is acceptable in sports and behaviors that cross the line. Your handling of this situation will be important in terms of both helping the athlete control himself and establishing team norms for behaviors that must be adopted by all of your athletes. Being consistent in how you react to an athlete's negative aggression is key. However, if you are unable to control an athlete's aggression, you might want to refer that individual to a sports psychologist so that he or she can get help with the development of nonaggressive coping strategies.

WHAT BOYS AND GIRLS WANT FROM A COACH

Another area in which we see similarities between boys and girls is in regard to their preferences for their coach's behaviors. When considering coaching behaviors, irrespective of gender, adolescent athletes care most about the coach's ability to demonstrate and teach the skills of the sport and to offer opportunities for competition and success. When adult athletes were questioned about their preferences for coaching behaviors, again there were no differences between men and women, with both expressing a preference for coaches who offered positive feedback, provided good training and instruction, and taught using a democratic style of leadership. There is some evidence to suggest that some boys prefer their coach to put an emphasis on fitness, competition, and achievements while some girls prefer their coach to make sure athletes stay active during practices (Martin, Dale, and Jackson 2001). However, these preference differences are so small that they shouldn't really guide your coaching. Rather, you should take note of the fact that athletes in general want a coach to teach the sport while keeping athletes active during practice.

....

KEY POINT *Boys and Girls Want the Same Things from Their Coach*

Boys and girls want their coach to

- design good practices that teach them the skills and tactics of their sport,
- provide positive feedback to help them improve,
- give them the opportunity to compete and demonstrate their abilities, and
- keep them active during practice in ways that lead to increased fitness.

....

COMPETITIVENESS

Previously, we discussed negative forms of aggression that we do not want to see in our athletes because they have harm as a primary goal. In contrast to negative aggression is positive aggression, which is physical behavior that carries the risk of causing harm but that does not have harm as a primary goal and is allowed within the rules of the game. Many people may think of positive aggression as competitiveness or assertiveness and is something that we typically do want to see in our athletes. That is, we want our athletes to dive for loose balls, to be willing to make hard tackles, and to go hard into 50/50 challenges (that is, where two players have an equal opportunity to get the ball).

....

SCIENTIFIC EVIDENCE *Differences in Boys' and Girls' Competitiveness*

Scientists asked nine- to ten-year-old Israeli boys and girls to run forty meters twice with the goal being to run as fast as they could (Gneezy and Rustichini 2004). The children in one group ran the distance individually both times. The children in the other group were matched with a person who had a similar time on the first run. They were matched regardless of sex, so some children were running with a child of the same sex and some were running with a child of the opposite sex. Because boys ran much faster when running "against" a partner, the scientists concluded that boys were more motivated by competition than were girls (see table).

RAN INDIVIDUALLY BOTH TIMES		MATCHED WITH A PERSON WHO RAN A SIMILAR SPEED	
Boys	**Girls**	**Boys**	**Girls**
Ran ~4 seconds faster second time	Ran ~4 seconds faster second time	Ran ~16 seconds faster second time	No improvement second time

....

Coaches who have worked with both male and female athletes often perceive that women are less willing than men to be competitive. At the collegiate level, former U.S. Women's National Team coach and current University of North Carolina at Chapel Hill soccer coach Anson Dorrance initially started out coaching men but then switched over to coaching women early in his career. In his book *Training Soccer Champions* (Dorrance and Nash 1996), Dorrance talks about the need to create a culture of competition for women so that they feel comfortable competing against one another and so that beating one another in practice becomes normative. He did this very effectively at the University of North Carolina, where he created charts allowing the athletes to compare their performance with one another, where he produced a series of small-sided games to keep competition going outside of the regular season, and where he emphasized the need to always compete against one another to further the improvement of the team.

Although there is some evidence that boys are more motivated to compete than are girls, it is important to remember again that individual differences are likely to be larger than differences between the group averages. You may have a boy or girl on your team who is extremely competitive, and you may have a boy or girl on your team who shies away from competition. In fact, I was asked once to work with a thirteen-year-old female athlete who was struggling socially on her soccer team because she was super competitive and was not well received by her less competitive teammates. In this scenario, I had to work with both the competitive athlete and her team to establish commonly accepted norms for behavior that allowed for competitive play. The key for you is to recognize which children need some guidance with regard to being comfortable with competition and always trying their hardest. If you can remind your athletes that they are really competing against themselves and trying to improve their own performance, you can help them to give 100 percent, whether performing individually, in a pair or group, or with a team.

In addition, the extent to which boys and girls are competitive is likely to be dependent upon the level at which they are playing. At the recreational level, these gender-based differences in the willingness to compete might be more evident. But as you move to higher levels of performance, it is more likely that the boys and the girls will be equally competitive. The techniques that Coach Dorrance used to enhance competition among his athletes would likely be equally effective and valuable if used with male athletes.

COMMUNICATION STYLES

Some evidence indicates that there are differences in preferred communication styles between men and women. You might have seen the popular book *Men Are from Mars, Women Are from Venus*. This book tells us there are observable differences in communication styles between men and women. However, there is no evidence with respect to communication style preferences between boys and girls or specific to communication within sports experiences. Although future evidence may show that communication preferences for children are not the same as for adults, our only choice at this point is to consider what we know for adults as one way of possibly informing our coaching of youth athletes.

Before discussing these sex-related differences, it is important to point out that criticism can be delivered in two forms. Destructive criticism is critical feedback that goes so far as to diminish the recipient's self-esteem or pride. By contrast, constructive criticism is carefully worded so that feedback is critical but includes solutions or ways to improve. As you might surmise, there are no sex-linked differences in how people receive destructive criticism—no one wants to be criticized in ways that are purposefully hurtful. However, for constructive criticism, we do see sex-related preferences for how this is delivered. For adults, women tend to prefer that constructive criticism is provided in private rather than in front of others. By contrast, men tend to be motivated by constructive criticism and are less concerned with the setting in which that criticism is provided. You'll notice that in both of these statements, I use the word "tend." This is purposeful and is meant to convey that this will not necessarily be true for all of your athletes but is a tendency across the gender group. As such, it will be important for you to figure out quickly which athletes are comfortable with and motivated by criticism being given publicly. It will be equally important to identify those athletes whom you need to pull aside to offer the constructive criticism more privately. If you can figure this out, you will be able to judiciously provide feedback in ways that best match the preferences of your individual athletes.

It is also true that women are more hesitant to offer constructive criticism to one another. You might notice on your team that it is challenging to get the female athletes to offer feedback to one another and that the feedback, when offered, is not well received. If you are coaching boys or girls and you want them to offer constructive feedback to one another, you must give them guidance about what this means, when it is appropriate to offer feedback, what kinds of feedback are acceptable, and how to receive that feedback. Importantly, men are quicker to offer constructive criticism, which may have a negative effect on team cohesion if it is not properly perceived by other athletes. As the coach, it is essential that you make clear your expectations for how critical feedback should be offered and received by the team. You will then want to monitor the giving and receiving of critical feedback to ensure that things stay positive between teammates. This is a difficult challenge for young people and will require that you provide them with the skill sets to both offer and receive critical feedback from their peers.

PHYSICAL PERFORMANCE

Prior to puberty, the differences that you see in terms of physical performance between boys and girls will be relatively small. In fact, there is no physical reason to separate boys and girls in sports until after puberty. When children are quite young, performance can be indistinguishable based on sex. For a short period of time just before puberty (nine to twelve years), girls may actually be more physically capable than boys because of their earlier maturation. Once puberty kicks in, boys will begin to gain an advantage in terms of strength, speed, and power. In adulthood, women are 70–80 percent as strong as men of the same weight (Miller et al. 1993). In sprinting events, the differences in speeds for the top six finishers in 283 sprinting events gives men an advantage of approximately 12 percent in their times (Seiler, De Koning, and Foster 2007). However, in many games, adjustments to the game are made to account for gender differences in physical attributes. For example, in golf the tee box often contains three sets of tees (set at different distances), in basketball there are different goal heights and ball sizes, and in gymnastics the events for men and women are different. These adjustments are designed to make the challenge appropriate relative to the physical attributes of the athletes. But it isn't clear that these differences in physical attributes should have any bearing on your behavior as a coach. As long as you understand what your athletes are capable of, you should be able to coach them effectively.

KEY QUESTION *Should Physical Differences between Boys and Girls Impact Your Coaching?*

Physical differences between boys and girls don't typically affect their ability to perform in sports until after puberty. Prior to puberty, boys and girls who are at the same skill level can compete together. After puberty, these physical differences will affect how you coach only in terms of your need to understand what boys and girls are physically capable of.

Prior to puberty, boys and girls can compete together, which provides benefits for all of the kids. *Illustration by Dominy Alderman.*

INJURY RATES

Another place where there are real differences between boys and girls is in terms of injury rates. In athletes playing the same sport, girls are at greater risk of head injuries than boys, and in response to head injuries, they have cognitive deficits and outcomes that are more severe than those of boys (Dvorak, McCrory, and Kirkendall 2007). Regardless of gender, if you have an athlete whom you suspect has experienced a head impact, that athlete should come out of the activity right away. If there is even the slightest chance that the athlete has sustained a sub-concussive or a concussive blow, that athlete should not participate again that day unless he or she is cleared to do so by a medical professional. If you are working with female athletes, recognize that the healing process may take longer for them and be patient as they take the time they need to recover. If you want more information on concussions, I encourage you to complete a concussion training course (see Resources).

Girls are also two to eight times more likely to have an injury to their anterior cruciate ligament (ACL) than are boys (Yu and Garrett 2007), and this risk increases during the teenage years. Although sports medicine professionals are working to develop training protocols to help minimize the risk of ACL injuries, at this time we know only that strengthening the hamstrings and core, stretching to ensure equal flexibility on both sides of the body, and being properly hydrated can help to reduce risk. So, if you are working with teenage female athletes, their heightened risk of an ACL injury suggests that you should prioritize teaching them how to strengthen their hamstrings and core and to stretch properly and encourage them to drink plenty of water at practices and games. This may help to reduce the likelihood of an ACL injury.

INJURY RECOVERY

When athletes are recovering from an injury, certain gender differences have been observed. Again, the information that we have comes only from college athletes, but these results suggest some gender differences that might be relevant to coaching youth athletes. Female athletes tend to rely on greater emotional support when recovering from an injury than do men (Mitchell et al. 2007). Hence, if you are working with female athletes, it is particularly important for you to express compassion about their injury and to stay in touch with them throughout the recovery process. Also, injured female athletes can perceive their coaches as being very negative toward them during the recovery period. This may be because they desire more emotional support than they are receiving from their coaches. Think about it from the perspective of an injured athlete. If you don't check in with that athlete regularly, what will she think about how much you care for her? She may infer that you don't care about her as a person because you are focused only on the healthy athletes who can directly help the team. Although it may be more important for girls than for boys, regardless of the sex of your athletes, you should keep up with their progress in recovering from injuries.

Why This Matters

Although there are some instances where gender differences might impact you as a coach, you are much more likely to see differences between individual athletes that are linked to their specific personalites than you are to see overarching differences that distinguish boys' teams from girls' teams. In fact, let me give an example using height to make this point. Although we know that the typical adult male is taller than the typical adult female, what we sometimes forget is that there is substantial overlap in the heights of men and women. That is to say, it is obviously untrue that all men are taller than all women, just as it is obviously untrue that all men are more competitive than all women. If you

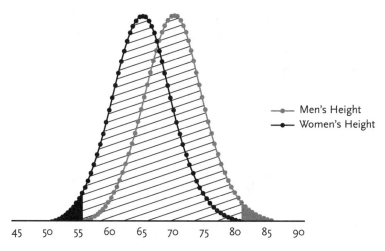

Distribution of men and women with respect to height

— Men's Height
— Women's Height

45 50 55 60 65 70 75 80 85 90

Graph 6.1. Height distribution for men and women in inches.
The substantial overlap of men's and women's heights is analogous to how
similar men and women are physically, psychologically, and socially.

look at graph 6.1, which shows the actual average height for men and women but assumes the same variability in height, you see that the average man (70 inches tall) is taller than the average woman (65 inches). But, you will also notice that most men and women fall in an area where there is substantial overlap in height (the shaded section) and only a small number of women are shorter than all men (solid areas) and an equally small number of men are taller than all women. This analysis can be applied to all the variables discussed in this chapter. So, for example, although there are small differences in competitiveness and communication-style preference between boys and girls, the majority of the athletes you coach will be similar in terms of how competitive they are and how they want their coaches to communicate with them. Hence, although gender-based stereotypes clearly exist and there is a societal bias suggesting that girls need to be coached with an eye toward potential "issues," our current understanding of gender differences is that there are few that should affect how you coach your athletes.

Activity

Despite the plethora of societal evidence of gender differences, the evidence does not support any large differences between boys and girls that should influence your coaching. That being said, there are a few places where the slight differences between boys and girls and between different personalities on your team might be worth considering in terms of your approach. For each of the following situations or topics, think about the personalities and/or gender of your athletes and explain your best approach.

1. RISK OF INJURY

_____

_____

_____

2. SELECTION DECISIONS (IDENTIFYING STARTERS/NONSTARTERS)

_____

_____

_____

3. DECISIONS REGARDING STYLE OF PLAY

_____

_____

_____

4. ALLOWANCES FOR SOCIAL INTERACTIONS

_____

_____

_____

5. INTEREST IN DEVELOPING THEIR COMPETITIVE SPIRIT

_____

_____

_____

CHAPTER SEVEN

Youth Sports Parents

As coach of a youth sports team, you will clearly be interacting with parents. These interactions can run the gamut from being very positive to being extremely negative. Undoubtedly, you've seen the clips of crazy parents attacking one another during or after a sporting event. Many believe that sporting parents have lost control and are ruining sports for the children. This is clearly an exaggeration and is influenced by small numbers of out-of-control parents. However, it does illustrate why it is important for you to consider the role that parents play and to identify ways to help them be supportive of their child's sports experience.

Given that more than 90 percent of youth sports coaches are parent volunteers, chances are that in addition to being a coach, you are also a parent of a youth athlete. So that means that you have some experience being on the sidelines or in the stands while your child is performing. You know it can be frustrating and exhilarating, maddening and joyful. The emotions that you experience during a sporting event may then be expressed in behaviors that range from positive to negative. Now, as the coach, you will want to think about parents from a different perspective, which may alter how you view the feedback, guidance, and support that the parents provide. Furthermore, in addition to working directly with your athletes, you will also be interacting both directly and indirectly with their parents. So, it is important to consider the role that parents play in youth sports.

Of course, parents are critical to a child's involvement in sports. Without their support, children would not be playing. The parents must sign the child up to participate, pay the necessary fees, purchase equipment and uniforms, and secure transportation to practices and competitions. Parents are also physically present in varying degrees at practices and competitions. And their level of engagement when they are present ranges from totally disengaged to highly involved, from positive and supportive to negative and critical. As the coach, you have the opportunity to exert some control over the types of feedback that parents provide, at least when they are at your practices and competitions. Getting off on the right foot with the parents is important because they will affect your experiences as a coach and because the nature of their involvement will also affect the athletes you are coaching. Furthermore, if you can help the parents recognize the value of being supportive influences on their child's sports participation, you will enhance the experience for everyone.

Starting on the Right Foot

One of the first things I would suggest when you begin working with a new group of athletes is to contact the parents right away to introduce yourself. You might do this in an email or in a parents' meeting before the first practice. In this introduction, you should describe your sports playing and coaching background, identify your profession, mention whether you have other children who are involved in sports, explain why you are coaching, and lay out your goals as a coach. You should also talk about your philosophy regarding practice commitment, playing time, and methods of communication. In addition, you should provide the parents with codes of conduct established by the organization. If your organization doesn't have its own requirements for parents, I would encourage you to talk with your organization's director about establishing your own team rules for parents. You might create these on your own or adapt rules created by others to use for your team. The National Alliance for Youth Sports offers the *National Standards for Youth Sports*, which provides a great starting point (see Resources). By setting appropriate expectations for parents prior to the start of the season, you will go a long way toward creating a climate that is conducive to learning, consistent with your aspirations for the athletes, and beneficial to the athletes.

The Parental Presence

Given that we are discussing parents of the athletes you are coaching, we already know that they have made a commitment to their child's participation in sports. What we must consider next is to what extent they are further engaged in the child's experience. The parents have a huge influence on their children's enjoyment of their participation through the reinforcement and feedback that they provide, and this will vary incredibly from family to family.

Parents' participation at practices exists upon a continuum, but you can think of them as falling into one of three categories: the drop-off parents, the present but uninvolved parents, and the participating parents. The drop-off parents typically bring their child to the practice site, drop him or her off, and return for pickup at the appropriate time. With drop-off parents, it is important that you make sure you have their current contact information so that you can reach them if their child needs them (for example, if there was an injury) or if they have not returned before practice ends. The present but uninvolved parents stay at the practice but are focused on other things and do not pay much attention to the practice itself. Such parents might converse with others, spend their time on the phone, read a book, or watch the practice, but typically they do not interact with you or the athletes. These two categories of parents are great for you as the coach. They are clearly supporting their child by making sure that the child is present at practice, but they are allowing you to work with their child without their direct involvement. Such a situation is ideal, and you should encourage these behaviors in your parents because they give the young athletes the space to learn and grow in their sport while focusing on the input from the coach.

The participating parents are those who watch the practice closely and offer their own input and feedback to their child during practice. Although such input and feedback can be objectively positive or negative, it will almost always have a negative effect on the child. This is because the parents' role is *not* to be involved at this time, and therefore their comments are almost certain to have a detrimental effect on their child. Even if the parents are trying to be helpful, this is not likely to be the result. For example, if these parents give improper instruction or instruction that runs counter to your own directions, the child is put in a difficult position. How is the child supposed to respond when given instruction from his or her parents that is not consistent with what the coach is saying? Parents' negative or critical feedback will be hard on the athletes and will influence their behavior since they do not want to disappoint their parents. For example, if an athlete tries a new move and is not successful and the parents make a disparaging comment, the athlete will be influenced not to try that new move again. Even parents' accurate direction and positive feedback will still have a detrimental effect on the athletes. This is because the parents are distracting the athletes from the coach, and ultimately the athletes will have a harder time learning to perform independently of their parents in the sport.

In a very general sense, the parents should not be engaging with their children at practices for several reasons. First, this is your time as coach to provide feedback and guidance to the athletes. Second, parents' feedback will likely make the child stand out as different from his or her teammates and may make the child self-conscious. Third, this is the time when children need to be able to try new things and to fail so that they can ultimately improve. If the parent is providing feedback during practice, it will likely limit the child's willingness to risk failure in practice. So, your coaching experience will likely go much more smoothly if you inform parents in advance that they should not engage with their children once practice begins. If you have a parent who is super-engaged during practices, you might invite that parent to serve as an assistant coach (if he or she has the skill sets and if this would be a good addition for all the athletes), or you might tactfully encourage the parent to allow his or her child the space needed to learn the sport. I have been to several practice sessions where there are no parents around at all. At a regional soccer camp at the Olympic Training Center in Chula Vista, California, I noticed a group of adults on a distant bluff who appeared to be watching the practice through binoculars. I asked one of the coaches whether those were visitors to the Olympic Training Center. The coach laughed and replied, "No, those are the parents. These kids need a break from them every now and then."

Fortunately, most parents will be disengaged during practices, and you are not likely to run into the participating parent. However, the exact opposite is true during competition. Even the most mild-mannered of moms and dads will often express their exuberance for the game frequently and loudly when watching a competition. I'm sure that they are well-intentioned and believe that they are supporting their child and the team with their comments. But for many the tone of voice or the content of what they say may strike their children and other children as being inappropriate. It is important to recognize that the parents can either contribute to the enjoyment of the event or lead to the experience of pressure and negative emotions by their children or by other children at the competition. Although I do not believe organizations will

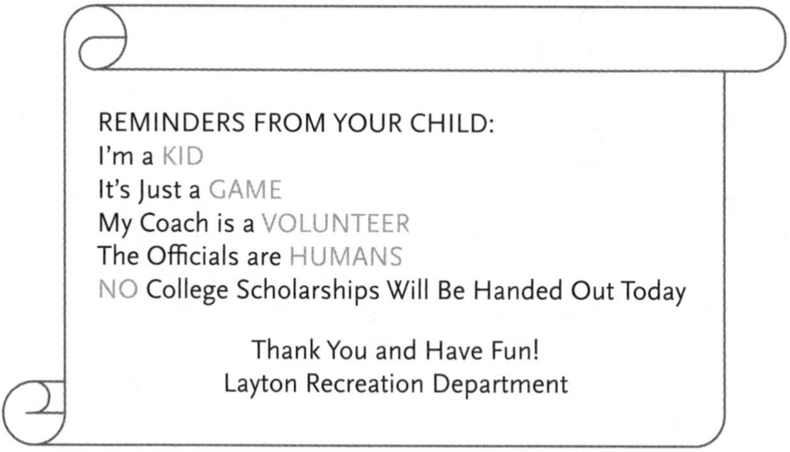

REMINDERS FROM YOUR CHILD:
I'm a KID
It's Just a GAME
My Coach is a VOLUNTEER
The Officials are HUMANS
NO College Scholarships Will Be Handed Out Today

Thank You and Have Fun!
Layton Recreation Department

Figure 7.1. Sporting venues across the country are posting signs to remind parents to keep youth sporting events in perspective.

ever completely ban parents from attending competitions, many youth sports organizations have attempted to control the parents' access to the children during competition by requiring that they sit on the far side of the playing field or court. This undoubtedly helps to some extent, but obviously many parents have loud voices that can be heard across the entire playing area. And at times the athletes will likely be performing in close proximity to their parents. Some leagues have posted signs to help remind parents of their role and of the fact that they are spectators at a youth sporting event (see figure 7.1). Although steps are being taken to encourage parents to demonstrate appropriate behavior at sporting events, these steps are not always effective. And it is important to remember that parents' behavior as spectators at competitions can have a powerful influence on youth athletes.

The Parental Influence

One way in which parents influence their children is that they provide an interpretation of the child's experience. They have essentially unlimited access to their children and so can provide these interpretations before, during, and after every practice and competition. Think about this very common scenario. Before the competition, parents drive their kids to the event and remind them how important it is that they perform well today and that lots of people will be watching. During the competition, the parents yell words of encouragement and reinforce good performance, but they also yell their child's name with a frustrated tone when the child makes a mistake and holler at the official to make the right call. When the child finishes the competition, the coach meets with the athletes and shares his or her perspective of the competition and their performance. The coach points out the positives of the competition, reinforces evidence of sportsmanship and effort that were displayed, and encourages the athletes to feel proud of their performance. Then the child gets into the car with his or her parents where he or she is literally seat belted in with no chance for escape. That's when the parents begin to offer their own perception of the competition and of the child's specific performance. If the parents offer positive reinforcement of mastery successes, express confidence in their child's competency following the competitive event, and have generally positive relationships with their child, the child will have enhanced perceived competence, enjoyment, and motivation (Babkes and Weiss 1999; Ullrich-French and Smith 2006). However, if the parents express disapproval or put excessive pressure and expectations on the child, the child will experience a decrease in self-esteem and self-confidence and an increase in anxiety.

KEY POINT *Children Know What They Want*

Children know how they want their parents to behave. They want their parents to be supportive, which means

- being silent and attentive,
- cheering when appropriate (for all athletes and for both teams), and
- offering praise and empathy.

What is interesting is that children know how they want their parents to behave at their competitions but may be unable to talk to their parents to share their perspective. One study of youth athletes suggests that children see their parents as fitting into one of three categories, described as the supportive parent, the parent who acts like a demanding coach, and the parent who acts like a crazed fan (Omli and Wiese-Bjornstal 2011). The youth athletes in the study indicated that they preferred supportive parents, which they described as parents who exhibit positive behaviors and give positive feedback. Some athletes said that they were also okay with parents who acted like demanding coaches, but most said that this was not their preference. None of the children liked parents who act like crazed fans. This research tells us that children recognize the supportive behavior that they want to see from their parents, and encouraging such behavior is one way you could make a huge difference as the coach.

....

SCIENTIFIC EVIDENCE *Parents and Children Have Different Perceptions*

A recent study (Sappenfield 2019) conducted with children eleven to twelve years old who were participating in a youth soccer league yielded some fascinating results. Parents and their children were asked to rate the extent to which the parents offered direction, gave praise or expressed understanding, and talked to them on the car ride home.

The following are the results:

- Parents perceived that they gave less direction than their children perceived.
- Parents perceived that they gave more praise than their children perceived.
- Parents perceived that they talked less about the game on the car ride home than their children perceived.

It is critical that parents find out what their children think about their behaviors before, during, and after competitions so that children are getting what they want and need from their parents in terms of support.

....

At the start of the season, you could ask your athletes to write down a thought or two about how they want their parents and their team-mates' parents to behave before, during, and after competitions. Ask them to think about when and how they want their parents to interact with them before, during, and after games. Compile these thoughts and share them with the parents at a team meeting to express to them the importance of being supportive of their children's experience in ways that are consistent with the team's needs. If your athletes are like others who have been interviewed, they will express that they like supportive parents. Supportive parents are described as those who watch attentively and silently, who cheer at appropriate times, who offer praise and empathy, and who intervene only if they are concerned their child might be injured (Omli and Wiese-Bjornstal 2011). Interestingly, many parents are not aware of their own behavior. They will readily identify inappropriate behavior by "other" parents but often don't recognize their own negative behavior or its effect on their children. So, teach your parents to be supportive moms and dads who follow the advice of their wise children.

What You Can Do

In my own coaching experience, I was extremely fortunate in that most of my athletes' parents met the description of supportive parents. But I did have one or two parents who either acted as coaches on the sideline or who yelled at their child in ways that would not be considered supportive. One way that I attempted to control the effects of parents on their children was to limit their access. For example, when playing indoor soccer, where teams do not change ends at the half, I deliberately switched one player from the side of the field he played on in the first half to keep him on the far side of the field from his family for both halves. I did this every week because I felt the need to provide that particular player with some space from the harsh tone of voice and the constant advice being offered by his family. Other times, I have instructed the kids to do their best to focus on what we have worked on. I've explained to them that the parents are yelling to be supportive but that they might not be saying things consistent with our team approach. I've asked them to do their best to focus on our team approach rather than try to please the parents on the sideline. I've then had to share our approach with the parents in an attempt to get them on board with their cheers and instructions.

As most coaches do, I would also bring my team in for an end-of-game talk prior to releasing the athletes to their parents. Before they shook hands with the other team, I would remind them that this is a time to treat the other players with the utmost respect. I'd encourage them to shake hands, to look the other players in the eyes, and to tell them "Good game." (I instructed them not to say "GG" as a shortcut

In sports, some parents provide so much instruction
to their kids that it takes the fun out of the game.
Illustration by Dominy Alderman.

because I think this undermines the sincerity of their words.) After they shook hands with the other team, I would spend about five minutes talking with them, reinforcing the positives that I saw in the game. I would emphasize things that were in their control like their effort, willingness to work hard after a mistake, teamwork, persistence, and good sportsmanship. I might also identify some places where we could improve and would indicate that we would work on these things at the next practice. I would typically end by expressing excitement and pride at their performance. At that point, I would send them back to their parents, whom I had educated to also be supportive and to reinforce the positive aspects of the game.

So, in your own coaching, be cognizant of the effect that the parents have on your athletes. If the parents are having a negative effect, you will need to figure out ways to minimize that influence. You might do this through surreptitious or blatant means that limit their contact, through helping your athletes cope with the parents' input, and through teaching parents to modify their behavior. When you get moments with the team to offer your own take on the competition, be sure to offer a positive, supportive interpretation regardless of outcome. Focus on things that are in their control and that you would like to see repeated. Identify shortcomings in the competition but acknowledge that those shortcomings are controllable and that they can be addressed through upcoming practices.

Why This Matters

To recap, since you are coaching at the youth level, it is important to recognize the influence of the parents on the children. You need the parents, but they may also make your job more challenging. Their influence can range from positive and supportive to negative and maniacal. As the coach, your best option is to set the rules early for the parents in terms of your expectations for them and to educate them to be good sports parents. Hopefully, the organization you are coaching for provides rules or codes of conduct. However, if not, you can find examples through a variety of sources that will provide you with a starting point to create your own set of rules consistent with your expectations for the parents. Things to consider are how you want parents to behave at practices, how you want parents to behave at competitions, and how you want parents to interact with you. Explain these behaviors clearly to your parents and use your communication skills to ensure that parents consistently meet your expectations during the season.

Activity

The influence of parents can be felt by the athletes at practices and competitions. For each of these situations, it is a good idea to have your rules and expectations prepared so that you can set the standards for parents from the get-go. In addition, consider how you want parents to interact with you when they might feel upset with your decisions. Some suggestions appear below.

AT PRACTICE

1. Parents should ensure that their child arrives to practices on time and ready to participate.
2. Parents are welcome to drop their child off at practice but must leave their current contact information.
3. Parents are welcome to stay at practices but are asked not to interact with their children during training or breaks.

4. _____

5. _____

AT COMPETITION

1. Parents are encouraged to attend competitions but are asked to sit on the side opposite the team bench.
2. Parents are encouraged to be supportive of their child and other children while observing the competition.
3. Parents should not provide critical feedback or instruction to the athletes while they are competing or during breaks from competition.

4. _____

5. _____

COMMUNICATION WITH THE COACH

1. I look forward to communicating with you regularly regarding the logistics of practices and competitions.
2. I welcome all positive feedback.
3. Please wait at least twenty-four hours following a practice or competition to share critical or negative feedback. I will respond to this feedback at my discretion.

4. _____

5. _____

CHAPTER EIGHT

....

The Coach's Role in an Athlete's Decision to Quit

....

We have talked briefly about when and why athletes choose to quit playing sports. As a reminder, a large percentage of kids drop out of organized youth sports each year, and many children have dropped out of organized sports completely by the time they are teenagers. There are a number of reasons why children choose to quit participating, but the top reason is because they are no longer having fun. So, that is why *making sure kids are having fun has to be your primary goal as a coach*. You may have other goals for them, which is great. But if they aren't enjoying playing for you, and this causes them to choose to drop out of the sport completely, then clearly you have not met your goals as a coach. So, how do we help guarantee that kids have fun?

Hey Coach, This Is Boring!

This may sound incredibly simple, but the first thing you need to do is make sure that your practices are not boring. In fact, that is the minimal level of acceptability. What you should really strive for are appropriately challenging and fun practices. If the athletes believe that your practices are boring, then they are certainly not going to want to come to practice, and if they do come they are not likely to have much fun. So, how do you know if your practice is fun or boring? It's really quite easy—look at the kids. What are they doing? Are they engaged and trying hard in your practice? Are they focused on what you are asking them to do? If they are engaged, focused, and trying hard, then you can bet they are having fun. But if they are disengaged, are causing disruptions or appear to be distracted, or are not giving much effort, this is not their fault. This is your fault! Your sport is inherently fun, so make sure you keep it that way. Don't turn practice into work. If you engage the athletes in a fun activity, they will not be disengaged, disruptive, or distracted.

....

KEY POINT *Lines Are Bad*

Nearly every sport is vulnerable to being reduced to an activity where children wait in line for their turn. Remember, in sports, lines are BAD!!!!

....

One thing that drives me crazy is when I see a practice in which the athletes are either standing around the outside of an activity uninvolved or are standing in lines waiting their turn while only one kid gets to play. When the lines are long, this is torture for the athletes waiting their turn. Imagine it for yourself—what if you as an adult were asked to wait in line for several minutes before you could participate. Then, once you do participate, your chance is over and now you have to move to the back of the line to wait your turn again. It's like being at the Department of Motor Vehicles and waiting in line for a long time and then finding out that you are in the wrong line and that you get to stand in line again. It's not very fun, is it? Now imagine yourself as a kid being instructed to wait in line for a chance to play. The sad thing is that I've seen lines used in almost every sport you can think of—football, golf, soccer, volleyball, basketball, baseball, and tennis. You have probably seen this yourself. A coach is working with ten athletes and has them performing one at a time while nine others wait in line. Think about what this means from a fun perspective. Only 10 percent of the group is having any fun at all! The other 90 percent are waiting for their chance to have fun. Now consider this situation from a teaching perspective. You are teaching each individual for only 10 percent of the time that is available, and they are getting only a fraction of the repetitions of the skill that are possible.

When our boys were seven, we enrolled them in a golf clinic. The coach was enthusiastic and clearly knew a lot about the game. At the first practice, I had seated myself some distance away and was grading papers. Every once in a while, I'd glance up to see what the children were doing. Unfortunately, I found myself looking up increasingly frequently as I recognized that with every glance, the children were still just standing around. The coach had each golfer watching while, one at a time, the other golfers would take turns hitting the golf ball. There were ten children in the class, and when it was their turn, they got to hit three balls before moving to the back of the line. It was mind numbing! If I were asked as an adult to do something this boring, there is no way that I would agree to do it. So why in the world would you put seven-year-olds in this situation? The idea is to make the sport fun!

Although lines might be useful in an activity incorporating multiple specific starting positions, there is no reason why any line should ever have more than two to three athletes waiting their turn. So, what this means is that you as a coach need to plan your practice in advance to ensure this does not happen. From a teaching perspective, it is critical that you have identified learning objectives prior to the practice and that you take the time to design your practice to reach those learning objectives in a way that gives your athletes maximum exposure to the activities.

Let me provide an example of a simple fix that translates to many sports. Imagine that you want to teach your team of soccer players how to shoot the ball. An inexperienced or unprepared coach would line the kids up and then let them come forward one at a time to take their shot on goal, retrieve their ball, and return to the back of the line. But the technique of shooting does not require that you have a goal at all, and there are an infinite number of activities you can design to practice shooting with more than one player shooting at once. One example would be to pair the children up, set them across from their partner with plenty of space between players, and let them practice striking the ball back and forth to one another. Now, in a ten-minute period, instead of them getting to shoot for 10 percent of the time (one minute), they are getting to shoot for 50 percent of the time (five minutes). Plus, they are also getting to practice controlling the ball that is struck to them with power, they are motivated to be accurate because that saves them having to chase the ball, and they are getting multiple repetitions of the technique. Meanwhile, you have the opportunity to watch them strike the ball several times in a row so that you can offer feedback and instruction. Another solution is a more complex series of passes that involve multiple players setting up the opportunity for the shot. This situation is much more realistic as it relates to a game and also keeps more children engaged in the activity. By having multiple short lines,

Coach: Rather than using a single line that limits involvement to one athlete at a time and centers around you (top), create activities that keep as many athletes involved as possible (bottom). *Illustration by Dominy Alderman.*

it's kind of like the lines at Disneyworld. Each line is active and short, so you don't spend time fretting over the time it takes to get to the grand event! As long as you have something entertaining to look at, you can't really judge how long it will take to get to the front of the line, and you feel like you're making progress, so you stay happy and content.

Relevant to this point, it is also important to consider the fact that you are likely to be coaching athletes at different ability levels. To keep it challenging and fun for everyone, design activities that are appropriate for the athletes where they are. In my opinion, if the teams are put together properly, you should have athletes who can meet similar minimum levels of performance so that you can design your activities in ways that will challenge all of them (although performance may look different). Certainly, you wouldn't want small-sided games that pit a strong team against a weaker team. Rather, you should work to ensure that teams are relatively equal in ability level when you set up "scrimmage"-like activities. Also, you should make sure that in one-on-one types of activities, you don't allow stronger athletes to match up consistently with weaker athletes. These two examples fall under the same principle—they will be boring for the stronger athlete or team and not fun at all for the weaker opponent. Furthermore, neither athlete or team in these situations will have the opportunity to improve by being challenged by a competitive opponent. But, when you set up activities to work on specific techniques or tactics, you should be able to design activities that allow children to perform at their best level and to have some degree of success. If you do see an athlete who appears to have mastered the activity, ask that athlete to achieve a higher level of consistency, to try something new within the activity (like a new move), or to work on the nondominant side. If you are working with youth athletes, then I can guarantee that no one will perform perfectly, so everyone has room for improvement within your activities.

I'm Ready for Other Things

A second reason children might stop playing a particular sport is simply because they may choose to play other sports or to participate in other activities. As children enter adolescence, their options for extracurricular activities increase, including middle school sports, musical or drama activities, and student council. They may also be getting more involved in their community through volunteer activities or through part-time work like babysitting or lawn mowing. In middle school, children also have greater amounts of homework, perhaps necessitating that they pare down their extracurricular sports activities.

As a result, many adolescents will make decisions to drop some sports but to stay with one or two where they feel competent, have friends, and find enjoyment. This is a natural process as children have increasing independence in the selection of activities that feel good to them. The key point I want to make here is that if they are not choosing your sport (and if they are doing this in large numbers), that may mean the sport is not meeting their needs. If you, as a coach, can ensure feelings of competence and enjoyment and opportunities to socialize with friends, you increase the likelihood that the athletes will choose to stay with the sport you are coaching.

I'm Not Good Enough

Another reason that children drop out of a particular sport is that they start to believe they are not good enough. As I mentioned earlier, this is most likely to happen in the middle school years as children are beginning to self-evaluate in critical ways. Also, at this time, many kids are trying out, practicing, and competing in sports for the express purpose of playing at a higher level. So, some kids are explicitly told by the adults running the program that they are not good enough to advance or to continue to compete at a certain level. Obviously, this has a horrible impact on the youth athlete if he or she has made a true commitment to success. And how this is handled by the youth sports organization, the coaches, and the parents is critical if they care enough to ensure that the young athlete can recover from this devastating news.

I recently spoke with a parent of an eleven-year-old who was dropped four levels at the annual tryouts for travel teams. The young athlete was the brunt of verbal jibes from his former teammates, who had all stayed on their original team. Despite this dramatic change in levels for this athlete, the parent was not contacted by the youth organization or by the former coach with a forewarning or an explanation. If the player wasn't holding up his end of the bargain by working hard to improve and being receptive to the coaching he received, then this move might certainly have been merited (although the parents should still have been alerted in advance). But if the player was giving 100 percent and working hard with his team, then the mistake was someone else's.

Perhaps he was initially placed on the wrong team, which suggests that the talent identification system isn't working properly. Or perhaps the coach he was working with was not able to help the athlete progress. If the player was committed to doing his best and worked hard for the former coach and was still dropped four levels, then I think the organization should probably examine its selection processes and coaching. In any event, if the organization has the youth athlete's development as the priority, then it appears that adjustments should have been made prior to the annual tryouts, and certainly someone should have contacted the parents in advance to explain the situation and to discuss how to help the player cope with this loss of status. This is a clear indication of when the organization's failure to look out for an individual player resulted in a young athlete having a very negative and traumatic experience.

Other children come to their own decision (which may or may not be accurate) that they are not good enough and then self-select to drop out. You will find that kids drop out of sports thinking they're not good enough at every level—at recreational levels, on middle school or high school teams, and on travel teams. So, what would make a young athlete come to the conclusion that he or she isn't good enough? In my opinion, this is typically a reflection of kids being too focused on outcome and on comparing themselves with others. If we compare ourselves with others and have a goal of being the best, then pretty much all of us would drop out of everything we ever try because there is room for only one person to be the best. We have to help our young athletes recognize that the focus for them should be on their own personal improvement. We need to compliment and reward effort, persistence, risk taking, and performance gains. Everyone has the ability to improve, so if you can teach your athletes to focus on the enjoyment that comes from the activity itself, then this question of whether or not they are good enough becomes less relevant.

Think about this for yourself. What is an activity you cannot do right now? Maybe you can't speak Spanish, or you can't play the violin. So, right now you are clearly not "good enough" at this skill. But what if you started practicing this skill regularly? You would improve. And if you practiced regularly for a long time, you would improve dramatically, and one day would become competent at that skill. This is obviously not a sports example, but it's meant to illustrate that it is critical for us to help young athletes adopt a growth mind-set (see chapter 9) by finding joy in their ability to improve with practice.

KEY POINT *Help Your Athletes Maintain Confidence*

It is your responsibility to help your athletes maintain confidence. You do this by focusing on

- improvement (everyone can improve),
- process (process leads to outcome), and
- effort (effort is under their control).

Burnout

It might be surprising for you to think about the possibility that youth athletes would experience burnout, but burnout does occur even in young athletes and particularly in those who specialize early. Burnout is experienced when an athlete is emotionally and physically exhausted and has lost the will to continue participating in his or her sport. Burnout is difficult to measure because children drop out of sports for numerous reasons and sometimes simply switch sports. But overuse injuries are a precursor to burnout, and we have evidence that overuse injuries are high among youth athletes (46–54 percent of all reported sports-related injuries) and that injury rates among youth athletes are on the rise (DiFiori et al. 2014).

Burnout results from the long-term experience of ineffective efforts to meet excessive training and competition demands and typically results in an athlete dropping out of the sport. Remember earlier when I mentioned Jennifer Capriati? Jennifer is one of the most famous athletes to experience burnout. She began her professional tennis career when she was one month from her fourteenth birthday. She was ranked in the top ten in the world before she was fifteen. But after a first-round loss in the U.S. Open, she dropped out of tennis for fourteen months. Remarkably, Jennifer was able to recover from personal and tennis-related struggles to return to professional tennis and to achieve success by making it to the semifinals in four Grand Slam events and winning three Grand Slam events when in her twenties. But Jennifer's case is unusual. Most athletes who truly experience burnout do not ever return to their sport, even to play recreationally.

So, why does burnout occur? Typically, burnout occurs in response to overtraining, which is physical training that is too intense or prolonged for the athlete to properly recover between training sessions. The challenge for coaches who are working with elite-level athletes is to find the proper balance between training and recovery, which results in the body adapting in positive ways to achieve higher levels of performance. When done properly, this is called periodized training. Periodized training includes cycles of heavier training loads followed by recovery periods that allow the body to rest and repair. The goal is to use the training purposefully so that adaptations are timed to correspond with important competitions, allowing the athlete to be both fit and rested to increase the likelihood of peak performance.

....

KEY POINT *Reasons for Burnout in Youth Sports*

The possible contributors to athlete burnout in youth sports include

- starting at an early age,
- high training load,
- year-round training,
- pressures for performance,
- additional stressors, and
- time constraints.

....

Periodized training can be used to great effect. However, when done improperly, the body doesn't recover fully, and athletes fall into a cycle in which they no longer achieve previous performance levels. As a result, they experience fatigue and frustration.

If you are coaching at the recreational level, overtraining should not even be among the realm of possibilities for your athletes. You should be training at a level and frequency that provides sufficient time for recovery. But because there are other factors that contribute to burnout, it is possible that even a recreational athlete may burnout from sports in certain situations. And if you are coaching at a higher level than recreational, the possibility of burnout is increased because of the higher volumes of training.

Before discussing the additional factors that contribute to burnout, there are two important points to be made about burnout in general.

First, there is not an optimal training load that will be right for all athletes. Every athlete is different, and the workload that is ideal for one may be too little or too much for another. Second, the link between how hard athletes train and the ultimate level of success they achieve in sports is not perfect. That is, the athlete who trains the hardest or the most is not necessarily going to be the one who is the most talented or achieves the most success. Hard work is essential, of course, but working too hard puts athletes at risk for overuse injuries and burnout. Next, let's consider the other factors that contribute to burnout. They can be categorized as physical, logistical, social or interpersonal, and psychological.

PHYSICAL FACTORS

It is important to recognize that the nature of youth sports today has contributed directly to an increase in the impact of physical factors at the youth level. Youth athletes are entering organized sports at early ages. As previously mentioned, children are enrolling in organized sports as early as three years of age. Also, decades ago, most sports were played in specific seasons. Swimming, baseball, and softball were summer sports; football, soccer, and volleyball were fall sports; basketball and hockey were winter sports. Today, though, these sports are all offered year-round. So, instead of getting a break from their sports to try another activity, many athletes are playing one sport year-round; some even add on second and third sports during the year so they can pursue their other interests.

Another physical factor that may contribute to burnout is early specialization. Athletes are choosing to specialize in a single sport at increasingly earlier ages. Years ago, most youth athletes would play a different sport every season and might even try several different sports in a season during their childhood years. They would typically begin to narrow their sports commitments down only once they reached high school age. However, the message that is being forwarded to parents is that children need to specialize early if they want to have the opportunity to be successful in their sport. While this may be okay or even ideal for some youth athletes, for many others the lack of a break will contribute to their likelihood of burning out. We will discuss early sports specialization in more detail in chapter 10, but in general experts believe that there are only certain sports where early specialization is necessary for success and argue for athletes not to specialize until later years.

A final physical factor for us to consider is chronic fatigue. Many of your athletes may be experiencing fatigue as a result of their commitments and responsibilities and a lack of recovery time. Today's youth are often overextended because of their involvement in multiple extracurricular activities on top of their schoolwork. Children often participate in after-school activities (sports, after-care, drama, music, tutoring) that result in them getting home in the early evening. They may then have household responsibilities and homework that can keep them busy for another hour or two. After that, many children spend their remaining evening time engaged with media, either through watching television, playing video games, or using social media. The trouble with this schedule is that there is no downtime for the body and mind to truly rest, and by ending the day on a video screen, sleep itself is often delayed and interrupted. If you are concerned about the lack of energy you are seeing in your athletes, ask them about their sleep patterns and help them think about how they might change their behaviors to ensure they are getting enough rest. Definitely talk to them about ending their media time thirty to sixty minutes in advance of the time that they need to get to sleep and about making sure their phones or other devices are not in their bedrooms waking them up at all hours.

....

KEY POINT *Most People Don't Get Enough Sleep*

Age	Recommended hours of sleep
3–5 years	10–13
6–13 years	9–11
14–17 years	8–10
18–25 years	7–9

(*Source*: National Sleep Foundation 2015)

....

LOGISTICAL FACTORS

Logistical factors that contribute to burnout include travel and the related demands. At the recreational level, travel should not be a factor because your athletes are practicing and competing locally. But at higher levels, travel can become a factor as athletes who are seeking better training and competition may practice at locations farther from their homes and schools and may travel regularly to competitions outside of their city, state, and even region. Some athletes may choose to train with a team or club that is as far away as sixty minutes from their home. Clearly, the regular travel to these practices eats into the time that athletes might typically have for schoolwork and rest. Athletes who play for travel teams or who frequently compete at meets and events outside of their local area may be traveling two or more weekends each month. And teams like travel hockey regularly travel ten or more hours each way for youth tournaments. The longer travel for competition adds additional stressors such as not being able to sleep at home, eating on an irregular schedule and eating out, and being away from social support. The logistics of traveling for practice and competition will add to the overall load being experienced by the athletes and are important for you, as a coach, to be sensitive to.

As coach of a travel team, remember that your athletes need time to rest and recover from practices and competitions. Thus, you should consider canceling practices or having lighter practices following travel weekends. If you have athletes traveling to your practices, help them think about how to best use the travel time to ensure they are taking care of themselves. That may mean studying or doing homework in the car or using that time to rest their body and mind rather than being plugged into a video game or movie. Additionally, while traveling to competitions, encourage your athletes to use time between competitions in ways that serve this same purpose of helping them to either take care of their responsibilities or to rest. Socializing with friends may also be important during those times but shouldn't be the top priority.

SOCIAL OR INTERPERSONAL CONCERNS

The social support that children receive from their teammates, coaches, friends, and family is vitally important in their ability to manage their emotions and to maintain their sense of self-worth through the ups and downs of their sports experiences. When an athlete is beginning to experience burnout, remember that this can manifest in the form of overuse injuries or can be evident in the athlete's sports performance. If you notice an athlete struggling to reach normal performance levels or to recover from small injuries, this may be a sign that he or she is experiencing overtraining. If athletes' sense of identity is closely tied to their athletic performance, they can experience a real crisis of identity when their performance declines or they are unable to play because of an injury. If their sense of self revolves around their identity as athletes, then imagine what it feels like for them to be unable to participate or to no longer be able to perform as well as they used to. For young people, this may be a greater risk than for adults because they have not developed as many aspects of their identity as adults have. If you asked young athletes to list the top descriptors of who they are, the lists are likely to be relatively short. They might say that they are athletes, students, musicians, sons/daughters, and friends. Now, what happens if you take away the athlete identity?. If you are no longer playing your sport because you are injured or if you are no longer one of the top athletes on the team because you are going through a performance slump, imagine the crisis of identity you would experience. And if your friends are mostly your friends through sports and you are not practicing right now or aren't performing at your normal level, imagine how you might need the support of these friends but also would have trouble approaching them. If you notice this in your athletes, you must step in to express concern, to offer them a break, or to help them navigate the stressors in their lives.

Although you might be able to help your athletes avoid burnout, there is another point to consider. Imagine how the parents of a youth athlete, and particularly one who is at a high risk for burnout because of his or her level of competition, might react if their child is not reaching previous performance levels. Remember, the parents are heavily invested in their child's success in terms of their commitment of time and financial resources. The parents are also likely to be frustrated and upset by the performance slump. As a coach, it is imperative that you help the parents and the child to understand what is happening and to guide them as they take the appropriate steps to address the overtraining and burnout issues. Additionally, if you recognize that injured athletes are missing being a part of the team, figure out how to keep them involved. Invite them to continue to attend practices and games and give them a valuable role. At practice, perhaps they can be in charge of splitting players up for small-sided activities or can keep track of a pitch count. At games, have them keep statistics for important aspects of the game. Remember, there is some evidence that this is more important for girls than for boys, so be particularly sure to reach out if you are working with an injured female athlete. Keeping her engaged may help her to cope with her injury and will also benefit her by providing an opportunity to think like a coach and to watch the game from a different point of view.

PSYCHOLOGICAL CONCERNS

A major factor that contributes to the experience of burnout is the level of sports-related stress that a person is experiencing. There are multiple sources of this stress, but at its root are expectations for performance. Athletes who have success early on may come to expect this success to continue at the same level as they advance in their sport. These expectations may also be expressed by teammates, coaches, parents, classmates, and friends. The athletes are likely to experience pressure to meet these expectations, and when they are too high or unrealistic, athletes can feel enormously stressed. This stress then impacts the way that competitions are experienced. Instead of approaching competitions with a positive attitude and a desire for success, athletes who feel pressure to perform approach competitions with a negative attitude and a fear of failure. This then further affects their ability to perform. In fact, it moves the sense of positive energy to a sense of anxiety, which then makes the achievement of a good performance even more difficult. Help your athletes keep sports in perspective by reminding them that there are multiple important aspects of their identity, that they have friends and family who care about them as individuals, and that they can control only certain aspects of their performance, such as their effort, focus, and persistence.

Boredom is another psychological factor that contributes to burnout. Athletes can perform well only if they are enjoying what they are doing and having fun with their performance. Once sports begin to look more like a job than an enjoyable pursuit, in terms of required practices, fixed expectations, and limited rewards, the risk of burnout increases. You might wonder how athletes can possibly get bored when playing their sport. Athletes' boredom can come from structured, repetitious practices where there is little to look forward to. Think about what a normal practice looks like, where athletes perform the same warm-up followed by multiple repetitions of the same activities. When repeated day after day, week after week, and month after month, this routine may become boring to athletes, particularly when they begin to experience frustration with their performance. It is your responsibility to keep practices fun so that athletes experience joy while they are training for their sport. One way to do this is to give your athletes control over the warm-up or to let them select a fun activity to end the practice.

Last, remember that you are working with youth athletes. Kids! If they express concerns that suggest that they are not having fun, that the sport has become boring or more like a job, or that they simply don't care about the sport anymore, that is the time for you to be a friend to that athlete. Listen to their concerns. Empathize with what they are going through. Hear them without feeling the need to offer solutions. Sometimes if they simply have the chance to talk about what they are feeling, that can provide a level of coping for them. If talking about it isn't enough, then you will have to make adjustments to help that athlete regain his or her enthusiasm for the sport and the love of the game.

Why This Matters

You can do a lot to help minimize the likelihood of burnout in your athletes. It is critical that you recognize the impact of repeated high-volume practices on them. Use appropriate periodized training regimens that provide sufficient time for rest and recovery to allow your athletes to progress while also avoiding the overtraining cycle. Again, burnout is not likely to be a concern in youth athletes who have a good balance across their activities and who are not overextended. But if you are working with athletes who have specialized early and are committing solely to one sport and training at high volumes, burnout could be a real concern. Getting to know your athletes well so that you understand all of their commitments will help you to better recognize periods of time when they may need a lighter practice or even a break from practice. In addition, reinforcing the benefits of being well rested and of appropriately prioritizing the manner in which they use their discretionary time will help them learn skills necessary for balancing their multiple commitments.

Also, be sure to consider the psychological stress that your athletes are experiencing and do all you can to minimize this stress. As young athletes, they are also students who have expectations for academic success, young people who are navigating the trials and tribulations of growing into adulthood, and family members who have unique interactions with parents and siblings. Teaching them self-regulation skills (like relaxation, goal-setting, or positive self-talk; see Etnier 2009) will help them cope with sport-related and other stressors that they face. Furthermore, if you stay calm and even-keeled in response to the outcomes of competitions, this will promote the same responses among your athletes, which will further help them be emotionally stable across the course of the season.

As a coach, you should be familiar with the signs of burnout. These include impaired performance, mood disturbance, and increased effort during training. If you see these signs in your athletes, the immediate response should be to lighten their training load. Another positive response would be to offer a change of venue or a change of activity. For example, if you are training swimmers, you could replace swimming with other cardiovascular endurance activities like biking or running. If you are a soccer coach, you could play team handball or basketball for a day or two instead of practicing soccer. If athletes pass the overtraining stage and are moving into burnout, the solution is to give them a complete break from training. Most coaches and athletes are loath to do this, but if athletes are on the brink of burnout, this is really the only thing that will help them. A true break from their sport will allow them to restore their energy fully, to remember the fun in their sport, and to actually miss playing their sport so that they have the desire to participate again. And, not surprisingly, they will regain their form quickly and will surpass the plateaus in performance that were so evident when they were overtrained. The alternative is to continue to push the athlete, which can have devastating consequences: it will only increase his or her risk for injury and burnout.

Activity

1. Think of an activity in your sport that you've seen implemented by putting athletes in a line to perform one at a time. Now, describe how you could adapt that activity to get athletes out of long lines, to maximize repetitions, and to increase participation time.
2. You have a child on your team who is getting really upset at his practices. He is easily frustrated when he is not successful, and he often quits trying even during practice. You are concerned that he may end up quitting the sport completely. How might you help this athlete?

CHAPTER NINE

The Rock and the Tree

One of the most important ways you can help your athletes is by teaching them how to judge their successes and failures. The manner in which they do this will be determined by their motivational orientation. A person's motivational orientation is something that you can push toward being more positive.

Which Do You Want to Be: The Rock or the Tree?

All individuals have a motivational orientation that defines their approach to achievement opportunities. And their approach influences choices that they make within their sport. A person's orientation exists upon a continuum, and the endpoints have been described in many different ways, including outcome/mastery, ego/process, and fixed/growth mind-sets. Here I refer to the continuum that exists between the rock and the tree, and I tie in concepts discussed in *Mindset* (Dweck 2016), which is a wonderful read for adults working with children. The athletes you are working with will have their own achievement orientation such that each athlete lies somewhere along the continuum from the rock to the tree. Athletes who have a strong rock orientation believe that their abilities are relatively fixed and unchangeable. By contrast, athletes who have a strong tree orientation believe that their abilities can be changed through hard work and practice. These orientations develop over time in young people and are largely reflective of the type of feedback that they receive from parents. However, they can also be influenced by the particular reward system in which they currently perform, which is called the motivational climate. Before talking about how you can influence a person's motivational orientation, let's start first by thinking about how you can identify your athletes' orientation.

You will be able to ascertain your athletes' motivational orientation simply by observing how they respond to successes and failures in sports. Athletes' orientation affects their interpretation of, and reaction to, outcomes they experience in practices and competitions. "Rocks" attribute their successes to their high level of talent and ability and their failures to a lack of talent and ability. Rocks will also attribute failures to things out of their control that they believe restrict their ability to be successful. "Trees" judge that their successes are due to their strong work ethic and high levels of effort and that their failures are due to a lack of work prior to a competition and too little effort during a competition.

If your athletes experience a loss, ask them what caused the loss. You can learn a lot about their orientation from their answers. If they indicate that the loss was because of a lack of ability on their part, they may have a rock orientation. If they go further to say that the competition was better and will always be better, they definitely have a rock orientation. On the other hand, if they indicate that the loss was because they were not adequately prepared to compete or didn't give enough effort, they are demonstrating a tree orientation. If they suggest that their competition was better than they were on that day, they have an orientation that falls somewhere between a rock and a tree—they recognize that ability and talent are part of the equation but also acknowledge that these are not permanent characteristics and that on another day they may be successful.

As a real example, watching a soccer practice the other day, I quickly identified a young athlete (an eleven-year-old boy) with a rock orientation. The athletes had the opportunity to take shots on their coach, who was playing in the goal. Some of the athletes were successful, but the coach was able to save the vast majority of the shots. The first time this particular boy shot and missed, he shouted, "That wasn't fair. My foot slipped." When he shot again and the coach made the save, his reaction was, "Why are you trying harder against me than for everybody else?" Do you see why this is evidence of a rock orientation? In both cases, the athlete attributed the miss to something outside of himself. By doing so, he didn't have to accept responsibility for being a poor shot on that day. Neither did he identify the actual reasons for the poor execution, so he didn't recognize that there are ways to improve. The boy was doing

Table 9.1. "Rock" and "tree" orientations and their effects on behavior

FOCUS	
Rock	**Tree**
On outcome	On process
On beating others	On improvement

BEHAVIOR	
Rock	**Tree**
Unwilling to try new things	Willing to try new things
Unwilling to give 100% effort	Willing to give 100% effort
Prefers uneven competitions	Prefers to play someone equally matched
Unwilling to persist in the face of failure	Willing to persist in the face of failure

everything in his power to protect his strong sense of his own ability and was not willing to be accountable for poorly executed shots.

It is important that we learn to recognize the two extreme orientations because the consequences of these mind-sets are impactful. If athletes have a rock approach and are successful, then everything is fine because these successes contribute to the athletes' strong belief in their own ability and talent. But, if they have a rock approach and are not successful on a regular basis, their confidence can begin to erode because they interpret that these unsuccessful outcomes are due to a lack of talent. A series of losses can dramatically undermine rock athletes' confidence, which can then lead to a downward spiral.

Those with the tree approach are much more protected against the ups and downs of sports competitions. Tree athletes attribute their success to hard work and effort, which encourages more of the same. Tree athletes attribute their lack of success to not working hard enough or to needing to find a new strategy or tactic. If tree athletes want to be successful, they know that they need to work harder, give more effort in practices and competition, and identify strategies that will help them be effective.

Clearly, as a coach, it is better to be working with a group of athletes who are trees rather rocks. When working with tree athletes, you will see that they judge their successes and failures in ways that lead them to continue to work hard and give great effort. Their confidence in their own ability will be relatively stable, and they will focus more on improvement than on individual outcomes. Athletes who are trees will continue to grow (like a tree) and to develop their talents, abilities, and strategies. By contrast, when working with rock athletes, you will notice that their confidence goes up and down in response to outcomes in practices and competitions and that their effort wanes as their confidence is jeopardized.

The Role of the Coach

Although your athletes will come to you with an orientation that they have developed over time and that is somewhat stable, you can help athletes who have a rock approach move toward being more tree-like. To do this, create a motivational climate in practices and competitions that reinforces tree-like thinking and discourages rock-like thinking by focusing your attention and reinforcement on your athletes' hard work, effort, persistence, and improvement. Think about the long-term impact this climate will have on your athletes. If you get them to work hard, give high levels of effort, persist in the face of failure, and improve, the extent to which they will improve as a group over the course of a season or year will be remarkable.

Let me expand on this further. Sometimes when I watch practices, I see athletes, teammates, coaches, and parents focusing on the outcomes of their efforts rather than on the efforts themselves. For example, in sports that require athletes to take shots on a goal, positive responses from the observers are most evident when players make their shots and are not evident when players miss. Of course, making the shot is ultimately important, but when you are working with young athletes and are trying to teach them how to play the game, this is not the most important thing. Rather, the technique, focus, decision-making, and effort that go into taking the shot are most important.

Here is a more specific example. When my boys were eight, I finally gave in to their wishes to let them play organized basketball. I did my homework by contacting the league director to learn about the program's mission and the coaching education requirements. Although I was still hesitant, I enrolled them in the program and off we went. At the first practice, the coaches asked the children to shoot regulation-sized basketballs at a regulation-height basket. Because the children were small, the balls were big, and the basket was high, the only way that the boys could occasionally make the shots was to heave the ball up shot-put style. I was disappointed to notice that the parents watching gave huge shouts of support whenever the ball happened to go into the basket. But I recognized that the parents were not well educated with respect to what they should be rewarding and reinforcing in these young athletes. I was mortified, however, when I saw that the coaches were also applauding and giving high fives to the boys who managed to make their shots. Meanwhile, the young athletes who were attempting to handle the basketball properly could only shoot it about six feet high and were never even close to making a basket. Although they were trying to use proper technique, these efforts were met with stony silence from both parents and coaches. This is a dramatic example of how rewarding the outcome may not even make sense when the technique used to produce the outcome is incorrect. Such a situation is completely counter to what the coaches should have been doing and shows how the coaches (and parents) contribute to the motivational climate. By rewarding outcome instead of process, coaches create a climate that teaches the children to focus on outcome as well and, as in this case, do not deliver the appropriate feedback to the athletes.

....

KEY QUESTION *What Makes a Good Shot?*

- If an athlete gets the technique, focus, decision-making, and effort right, then he or she will have taken a good shot (whether it goes in or not).
- If an athlete takes good shots regularly, the ball will start to go in.
- In the absence of proper technique, focus, decision-making, and effort, the shot is bad, regardless of whether it goes in or not.

....

As another example, when I was a novice coach, I made a mistake that I think is quite common and could apply to a variety of sports. My first coaching opportunity was with a group of eleven-year-old girls. I asked my soccer players to try a technique called juggling, where each athlete would attempt to kick the ball up in the air repeatedly to herself. At the end of a try at juggling, I would ask the girls, "Who got the most [repetitions]?," and after some quick discussion, a proud hand would go up. By doing this, I was making the elementary mistake of focusing on outcome and a winner rather than on self-referenced improvement.

....

KEY POINT *Getting the Most Hands to Go Up*

- It makes no sense to ask, "Who got the most?"
- It makes great sense to ask, "Who improved?"

....

Now, as a more experienced coach, what I do over the course of several practices is ask the children to try to juggle without ever requiring them to count their juggles. They will of course be counting in their heads and may even express excitement as they notice themselves improving over time. I watch them and give feedback on technique and encourage them to keep trying. After several practices, I then ask them to count their juggles and let them try for several minutes. I ask them to remember how many they got and then instruct them to try again. After the second effort, I ask, "Who improved?" Do you see the slight shift in the focus and the effect it will have on the kids?

In the first example, when I asked who got the most, I ended up with only one or two (in the case of a tie) athletes feeling successful, and I was encouraging the children to compare themselves with each other. This makes no sense at all because I know that kids are all different and will have varying levels of success at juggling, depending on numerous factors that are not currently in their control. The only things that really are in their control are how hard they try, to what extent they focus on executing the skill properly, and how long they are willing to keep trying even when they aren't having much success. By asking who got the most, I was working against my own goals because I was encouraging those who were really poor at this skill to give up, since they would not be able to outperform kids who were dramatically better than them at that point in time. But by asking who improved, I could end up with 100 percent of the kids raising their hands to show me that they had improved. This is surely my goal as a coach. If all the children improve over time, then I have reached my goal. By asking them to self-reference and to focus on their own improvement, I allow every child to be successful, and I am encouraging them to continue to try hard, to focus on the skill, and to persist despite early failures because of the reinforcement they will receive from the coach.

Now, think about this exact analogy as it relates to winning and losing. If the only thing we care about at the end of a competition is which team got the most goals or scored the most baskets or got the most points, then only one hand (or team of hands) will go up. But, if at the end of every competition we asked who had fun, who tried hard, or who did something they are proud of, then we can get all hands to go up!

So, the key for you as a coach is to create a motivational climate in your practices and competitions that encourages your athletes to be trees. You want them to recognize that their ability levels can be improved with effort and persistence, that they will be rewarded for demonstrating improvement, and that outcome is valuable only when it comes in response to hard work, effort, and the demonstration of appropriate skill and technique.

Additional Implications

There are additional consequences of the rock and tree approaches that should be mentioned because of the implications for your athletes' progress. One consequence is that because rock athletes are very invested in outcome, they are unwilling to risk failure. This means that they will be less willing to take on challenging situations, to try new things, or to give their all when the outcome is in question. So, imagine for a minute that you are working with an athlete with a rock orientation. Let's take a look at each of these implications.

Because the athlete has a rock orientation, he is very invested in achieving successful outcomes because those outcomes protect his own view of his ability. This mind-set then impacts his willingness to take on challenges. Imagine he has the opportunity to compete in a one-on-one situation against another opponent. If this rock athlete could choose between someone who was much better, a little bit better, or much weaker, which person would he choose? The rock athlete's first choice would be the person who is weaker than him. The reason is that this guarantees success, which then ensures that his view of his own ability remains positive and intact. If that choice were not available, whom do you think the rock athlete would choose next? This answer is somewhat counterintuitive, but his second choice would be to compete against someone who is much better than him. By making that choice, his view of his ability is still protected. That's because no one would expect him to be successful against an opponent who is substantially better than him. So, think of the implications in terms of a rock athlete's opportunities to improve through competition. If rock athletes will always choose the weakest or the strongest competitor, they limit their ability to improve through challenging themselves against opponents who are slightly better than they are. In the end, they consistently choose to perform in situations where the outcome is guaranteed, and by doing so, they limit their opportunities to improve.

KEY POINT *When Does Competition Help Athletes Improve?*

Competition helps athletes improve only when they are competing against others of similar ability.

Rock athletes will also be unwilling to try new things. This is again because they are so invested in the outcome of their performance. Imagine that you have a rock athlete whom you would like to teach to be a switch hitter in baseball or a tennis player whom you would like to teach to play a serve and volley game instead of staying at the baseline. If you are working with rock athletes, they will be unwilling to try these new things because they will not be able to handle the initial failures that are sure to occur. Teach your athletes that failure is okay. The saying goes, "F.A.I.L. means first attempt in learning." This concept is something that is critical for our athletes to understand and be willing to experience if they have goals of improving in the sport.

KEY POINT *Failure Is Okay*

F.A.I.L. — First Attempt in Learning

Last, when rock athletes are performing, they will always be in tune with the momentum of the competition. If they are winning and having success, they will continue to play hard and to give effort to ensure they achieve their desired outcome. However, if they fall behind, they are likely to decrease their effort. The reason is because by decreasing

Athletes who have a tree orientation will ultimately be more successful than athletes who have a rock orientation. *Illustration by Dominy Alderman.*

their effort they can again protect their positive sense of their ability. If they lose, they can explain away the loss by saying that they didn't really try as hard as they could. This is a form of self-handicapping behavior that is designed to protect these athletes from the worst situation (from their point of view), which would be competing at their hardest and losing to an equally matched opponent. This form of self-protection can extend as far as feigning fatigue, suddenly developing an injury, or purposefully behaving in a way that results in a penalty or ejection from a match. These behaviors may seem counterintuitive, but if athletes are trying desperately to protect their positive perception of their ability, they are actually protective behaviors that allow athletes to attribute a loss to these alternative explanations.

You can help your athletes move toward being more tree-like in their approach. Create a mastery climate by recognizing and rewarding effort, learning, mastery, persistence, and improvement. Show the athletes that these concepts are important and encourage them to focus on these aspects of their performance. By getting them to concentrate on these things, you help them develop as athletes and teach them to find joy in their own performance and growth rather than relying on beating others, which will greatly help your athletes in the long run not only in sports but also in other achievement settings (like music, drama, and academics). Evidence clearly shows us that over time, athletes with a tree approach will outperform those with a rock approach.

Trophies

I am often asked what I think about trophies in youth sports. This is a tricky question because trophies do have an influence on motivation. In particular, trophies contribute to the motivational climate because they convey a message to the recipient. So, the questions we need to consider are these: Do trophies contribute to motivation in a good way or in a bad way? And what is the message that trophies convey? In a general sense, a trophy is an external reward that is meant to motivate athletes to do what is necessary to earn the reward. When athletes receive a trophy, it reinforces the behaviors they believe they performed to receive the trophy. So, this brings up an important distinction between the types of trophies that are typically given out in youth sports—participation trophies, trophies after competitions, and trophies after the season.

A relatively new phenomenon is the "participation" trophy. This award is given out to all competitors at an event, at a tournament, or at the end of a season. What are the behaviors that were performed to receive a participation trophy? If the trophy is given indiscriminately to every athlete, what is the message that is being conveyed? If this is truly a participation trophy that every athlete receives regardless of his or her specific/unique behavior, the message is that all you have to do is show up. From the perspective of the organizers of the event, tournament, or league, this may be precisely the message they want to convey. All you have to do is pay the fees to play, show up to some of the events, and you will receive a trophy. You don't have to work hard, you don't have to try new things, you don't have to compete, and you don't have to manage your emotions during a competition. You don't have to do anything except walk in the door. The problem with these trophies is that they deliver the wrong message.

....

KEY POINT *Participation Trophies*

What messages do participation trophies convey?

- All you have to do is participate.
- You don't have to work hard, improve, be a good sport, try your hardest, have a positive attitude, or anything else. Just show up!

....

Trophies are also used to reward top finishers in competitions. Maybe they are given to the first-, second-, and third-place athletes or teams, or maybe they go only to the winner. These trophies convey that the recipients are deserving of recognition for achieving the outcome of winning the competition. And that message may be of value to the recipients because it acknowledges the hard work, dedication, and effort that they put into practice and into the event itself. However, there are several important points to be made about these outcome-based trophies. One is that if the athletes become too focused on outcome, they can forget the reason they are competing in the tournament in the first place and can begin to think that winning the tournament is all that matters. For example, it is not uncommon today for teams who travel to tournaments and fail to qualify for the championship game to leave the tournament before playing their last game. That is, when asked if they want to play in their last group game or a consolation game, parents, athletes, and coaches decide that since the game "isn't for anything," there's no reason to play. Wow, does that ever fly in the face of the reasons for traveling to tournaments in the first place! The value of the trophy has come to replace the value of playing a game against an evenly matched team in a competitive environment. Winning the trophy has become the only reason for being there. Effectively, the goals for playing have now switched from playing for fun, experience, and competition to playing for the external reward of a trophy

A second point to remember is that if the athletes are competing on a regular basis in events in which trophies are given, the trophies can begin to lose their meaning. I've seen many young athletes' rooms filled with trophies and ribbons recognizing their top performances in numerous events. When I've asked them what a particular ribbon was for, often they can't even remember the event at which they won that ribbon. In this case, the trophies have lost their power to motivate athletes because they no longer convey any special meaning.

The third thing to think about is the notion of what is important in sports. If the athletes are playing in a tournament to win the trophy rather than to have fun competing against other evenly matched teams, then what happens when they don't win the trophy? If they care only about the trophy and don't win it, then suddenly the tournament was a failure and they may experience immense disappointment. If this happens regularly, then they may become less interested in competing at all. In this case, the trophy changes from being motivating to being the only reason to compete, and when it appears to be out of reach, the athlete loses interest.

··

KEY POINT *Tournament Trophies*

If your athletes are playing to win trophies,

- what happens when they don't win?
- what happens if the trophies come without much effort?
- what level of competition do they choose to play against?

··

Trophies or awards are also used at the end of a season to reward particular athletes for their performance. I've primarily seen these trophies awarded at schoolwide events for all school sports in a given season. Oftentimes, these awards recognize the athletes who have consistently performed the best across the season. So, I've seen award ceremonies where the awards for the cross-country team, which includes fifth through eighth graders, were given to the top two athletes (boys and girls) who were the fastest runners consistently across the season. In cross-country, this often means that they went to the four strongest eighth-grade runners. Think about what message this sends to the team. Those four athletes already know who they are—they already know that their times across the season were fast enough to be counted toward the team scores. By rewarding these athletes publicly, you are emphasizing that outcome is what is most important. Meanwhile, you are ignoring the factors that contribute to outcome and that you want to engender in *all* the athletes on the team. If you are an athlete on the team who isn't already a strong runner, then the coaches apparently have little to say to you for your efforts. By using the end-of-season awards in this way, you encourage your top athletes to continue participating, but you do nothing to encourage your other athletes to stick with the sport. Actually, you might not even be encouraging those top eighth graders to continue participating. If the same system of rewards is used in high school, it is highly unlikely that they will be the top runners next year when they are on a team that goes through twelfth grade.

....

KEY POINT *Use End-of-Year Awards to Reward Behavior*

If you have the opportunity to give awards at the end of a season or a year, consider using them to recognize behaviors that you want to see in the future. Some examples:

- Last to Leave
- Most Improved
- Mr./Ms. Positive
- Hard Worker

- Coach Jr.
- Rookie of the Year
- Helping Hand
- Love of the Game

....

If awards must be given at the end of the season, then they should be given to those athletes who demonstrate the behaviors that will ultimately help them achieve the desired outcomes. These awards might be for the hardest worker on the team, for the most committed athlete, for the athlete who improved the most across the course of the season, or for the athlete who was most encouraging to others on the team. These types of awards could be achieved by any athlete on the team (not just the one who is the most talented as a middle schooler) and would help motivate all the athletes to work hard and make valuable contributions to the team the following season. Ironically, these types of awards would contribute to the team as a whole improving so that you increase the chances of meeting the team goals of being competitive at events against other teams.

I'll never forget an example that my doctoral adviser, Dr. Dan Landers, shared with me that shows how an extrinsic reward can be used to control behavior in a way that you might not expect. In a small town in middle America, there was an older gentleman, Mr. Truff, who lived in a historic two-story home known for its beautiful traditional windows. Next door to this home was a large empty lot that attracted a group of neighborhood kids looking for a place to play baseball. Every Saturday these kids would get together to play, and they started to get pretty good. Once they got a little older and a little better, they began to regularly be able to hit the ball beyond the confines of the empty lot. This is where the trouble started. One Saturday, they hit the ball through one of Mr. Truff's windows. Now, these windows were not cheap, so Mr. Truff was extremely upset. But he was a psychologist who quickly recognized that he had better figure out a strategy to discourage this behavior. So when the boys came to the door to apologize and retrieve the ball, Mr. Truff said, "It's okay. I really enjoy hearing you all having fun out there on Saturdays playing baseball. In fact, I'll give each of you one dollar for playing today, and if you play next Saturday, I'll give you another dollar." This went on for about five weeks, with Mr. Truff shelling out ten to fifteen dollars every Saturday so that each boy had his dollar. When the boys returned on the sixth week, Mr. Truff said, "I'm sorry boys, I am not going to be able to pay you any more to play baseball." Do you know what the boys did? They quit playing baseball. Why? Because they wouldn't get a dollar to play anymore. So, since they weren't being paid to play, the young athletes decided it wasn't worth it. Do you see what Mr. Truff did? He changed the boys' motivation from being internal (originally, they were playing for fun) to being external (now they were playing for the dollar). It only cost Mr. Truff around sixty dollars to get the boys to stop playing baseball so that he didn't have to replace any more two hundred dollar windows!

Remember this story. The idea is that you want the kids to be internally motivated to play. You don't want them to play because you told them they have to or because their parents told them they have to. You don't want them to play for trophies or prizes, and you don't want them to care only about outcome. You want them to play because they want to play, to work hard, and to improve in their sport. Only those athletes who want to play for their own reasons and who can get joy from practicing hard, giving their all, and improving are likely to continue to play the sport. So be extremely thoughtful in how you offer external awards to athletes. I would strongly discourage you from using external rewards as a motivator for simply participating, for winning, or for being the best. If you want to use awards with your team, make sure that they are given to reinforce the behaviors that you want to see displayed by your athletes. And be sure to also teach them to give their best because it feels rewarding to them. Teach them to compete at their hardest for the sheer joy of knowing that they did just that. If they happen to win, that's great. But if they win without trying, that is not a success. Winning should feel good when it is the result of sustained effort, hard work, and devotion and when facing an equal or better competitor.

Who's in Charge?

This brings me to another important point that is related to the motivational climate that you are creating for your athletes. When you run your practice, whom do you want to be in charge? This may seem like a question with an obvious answer. But there are compelling arguments to be made for letting the athletes have some control in their practices. This is because when athletes have more control over their experiences, they will be more motivated.

A climate in which the athletes are allowed to have some control is called an autonomy-supportive climate because it supports the athletes' ability to be more autonomous or self-determined. In this climate, the coach acknowledges the athletes' thoughts and feelings and invites them to take part in decision-making. This is in contrast to a controlling environment in which the coach is authoritative and does not invite or value input from the athletes. Obviously, the creation of an autonomy-supportive climate doesn't mean that you give the athletes control over everything. It simply means that at appropriate times, you give them these opportunities. For example, in practices you might allow the athletes to self-select teams for one of the activities or decide if they'll take a water break after thirty minutes (of course, if it is really hot, you may need to mandate a water break at fifteen minutes!). Importantly, you may allow for more input and choice in certain situations but feel a need to be more controlling in other situations. That is okay! For example, you may be more autonomy-supportive during practices and even for parts of games, but in the last five seconds of a basketball game in which you've just called a time out, you may choose to be more controlling. The idea is to show the athletes that you value their opinions and input and to give them the chance to make some small decisions that will allow them to feel more self-determined and hence be more motivated (Amorose and Horn 2000; Hollembeak and Amorose 2005; Amorose and Anderson-Butcher 2007).

···

Autonomy-Supportive Climate	Controlling Climate
You offer the athletes choices	You make all decisions
You explain your rationale	You don't explain your thinking
You seek input from the athletes	You don't invite the athletes' input
You let athletes problem-solve	You tell athletes the answers
You focus on personal improvement	You focus on beating others

···

To create an autonomy-supportive environment, you should take several steps (Mageau and Vallerand 2003). First, allow athletes some freedom of choice. This doesn't mean that you let (or expect) the athletes to run the practice but rather that you offer choices within the structure of the practice. An example would be that you present two options for a warm-up activity and allow the team to vote on which they will do. Second, explain your rationale for your practice or for specific activities. In other words, you might say that based upon the last competition, the team needs to work on shooting and then briefly explain how the practice is designed to focus on that skill. Third, ask for input from the athletes on a regular basis. One time to do this might be at halftime or after a competition, when you could let the athletes first offer their perspectives on what the team has done well and where there is room for improvement before offering your own perspective. Fourth, provide opportunities for athletes to problem-solve. For example, when you set up an activity, rather than tell the athletes in advance how to solve the problem of the activity, allow the athletes to figure it out on their own. If the athletes are asked to play one-on-one, for instance, and they receive the ball (or puck) from a defender who is coming toward them from one side of the goal, let the athletes try the activity several times before stopping them and providing a relevant coaching point. The first coaching point might be that the athletes should take their first touch toward the side away from the defender. Let the athletes go for a while and then stop them to make the second coaching point. Maybe this point is that they should go to the goal the first time they beat the defender rather than slowing down or cutting back so that they have to beat the defender a second time. Similarly, when providing feedback, it is a great idea to let the athletes first critique their own performance. By so doing, you give them autonomy but also help them increase awareness of their own behavior. Last, consistent with the previous discussion, create a climate in practices and competitions that focuses on improvement and self-referenced behavior rather than on outcome. By doing all of these things, you are giving the athletes a voice and a sense of control over their experience, which can lead to increased feelings of investment in their sport.

After the Game

So, what should you say after a competition? As the coach, you will be the first adult to speak to the athletes after the competition. This is your window of opportunity to help your athletes deal with the emotions of competition and learn how to interpret the event. You can set the stage for how your athletes move from this competition into the next series of practices and the next competitions by what you say and do. By interpreting the event in a positive way, you help your athletes move on with the mind-set that they can use practices to improve in ways that will help them be competitive. It is critical that you use this time to model an appropriate response to and interpretation of the event.

Should what you say depend upon the outcome of the event? The simple answer is no. The outcome of the event should have very little impact on what you say to your athletes. Remember, winning is not what is important with youth athletes. What is important is how they played, their effort, the extent to which they executed the things you've practiced, and what they can learn from the competition.

Think about it. If your post-competition talk depends upon the outcome of the event, then you will applaud the victories and be upset following the losses. But how does this teach the athletes anything? Don't you think they recognize that they won or lost? Of course they do. So, if you focus exclusively on the outcome, you are not conveying any unique information to your athletes. You are also not doing anything that reflects your expertise as the coach or your responsibilities as the coach.

Regardless of the outcome, you should focus your conversation on the positive behaviors. Emphasize things like effort, hard work, recoveries from mistakes, changes in the momentum that benefited your team and the events that led to those changes in momentum, the use of proper technique, and good decision-making. Point out athletes whose hard work created opportunities for success. Note the things that were done right. After pointing out the positives, it is certainly acceptable to then identify two to three places where there is room for improvement. Again, this is true whether you won or lost! You can wrap up the conversation by again emphasizing the positives and indicating that you look forward to addressing shortcomings at the next practice. This is a perfect demonstration of using a sandwich technique to communicate some critical feedback between supportive comments.

· ·

EXAMPLE *Postgame Talk (Regardless of Outcome)*

"All right, this was an incredible team effort. I'm very proud of you for how you played. Let's think about the things we did well. Your defending was awesome. Payton and Sophie—your strong rebounding and quick release gave us opportunities for easy baskets. Charlotte, I love how you went hard for loose balls. You all worked together as a team and took good shots. We do need to work on our balance and squaring our shoulders, so we can start knocking those shots down. I'm really proud of you all and look forward to working with you next week to build from this point."

· ·

One behavior that is horrible to see in coaches after a game is blaming and shaming. I have seen too many coaches place blame on the athletes for a loss and then shame them for things like a lack of effort, poor communication, or a lack of focus. Remember, coach, you're the one who is teaching them how to perform in a sports setting. If you honestly think they're not giving enough effort, maybe you need to reinforce effort more in practice. If they're not communicating well as a team, then that's where you need to work with them. If you feel like there's a lack of focus or that they didn't execute well under pressure, how does it help to tell them that? If this is something you've worked on in your practices, then maybe you are frustrated that they didn't execute the way you expected. But remember, this is youth sport. These are young people trying to learn how to perform in a competitive sports setting. So when you talk with them about what you want to see, be specific. Remind them of what you want them to focus on. Ask them to reflect on where they execute well and where they have room for improvement. Ask yourself if you have really taught them to do the specific thing you are expecting to see. For example, how have you taught them to focus on the appropriate aspects of the competition? How did you train them to maintain focus throughout an event? To what extent did you set up gamelike situations to teach them to execute under pressure? It is unfair for any coach to berate the athletes for a loss unless the coach honestly believes they threw the competition just to upset and disappoint the coach and parents (heavy sarcasm here). My guess is that athletes do their very best and that their performance is a reflection of what they have been taught thus far. So, coach, after a competition, take responsibility for what you have taught or failed to teach your athletes.

....

EXAMPLE *A Coach Taking Responsibility after Competition*

Recently, I observed a coach communicating with his team members after they had lost three games in a soccer tournament by scores of 4–1, 5–0, and 5–1. The team was undefeated in its regular season, but the tournament included much stronger teams. The coach said, "Boys, these losses are not your fault. The teams we played are better than we are right now. If we won all the time, how would I know where we needed to improve? Now I know what we need to work on, and I know how to design my practices. And when we play them again, we'll be better." Now, that's an impressive way to handle a difficult tournament!

....

Why This Matters

Athletes will come to you with their own style of approaching achievement situations. This style can range from being very rock-like to being very tree-like. A tree-like approach will serve athletes better because this will allow them to handle successes and failures well and to engage in practices and competitions more positively. The motivational climate that you create in your practices and in competitions should encourage a more tree-like approach. By giving athletes some control over practices and inviting their input, you increase their commitment and investment. By rewarding the key factors in the process toward success, you help athletes learn to focus on those factors as well and ultimately help your athletes develop to their potential.

Activity

Consider these situations and offer ways you could respond using a tree approach.

1. Your athletes are working hard in an activity but aren't mastering the fine points you are trying to teach. How do you respond?
2. An athlete doesn't meet his or her performance expectations (for example, misses a shot, doesn't reach a performance goal, makes a critical mistake). What do you discuss with the athlete?
3. Your team is in a tournament and doesn't perform as well as expected. Some of the players and parents are lobbying to leave the tournament early rather than stay to compete in the final event/game. What do you say?

CHAPTER TEN

....

Early Specialization versus Diversification

....

The Controversy

A pressing issue that many parents and coaches wrestle with relates to early sports specialization. Should we advise athletes to specialize early by focusing exclusively on a single sport, or should we encourage them to try multiple sports in their early years? Those who argue for early specialization suggest that athletes (and their parents) choose one sport early (six to seven years of age) and participate in intense, year-round training with a focus on deliberate, purposeful practice rather than on enjoyment and play. Those who argue for sports diversification encourage athletes to sample several different sports during the early years and to specialize at a later time (typically in adolescence). Sports diversification proponents suggest that athletes should focus on enjoyment and play rather than on deliberate, purposeful practice.

Years ago, participating in high school athletics was an aspirational goal for young athletes who hoped to earn a varsity letter in one or more sports during their high school years. These athletes would play a different sport each season, striving for excellence in each. However, in recent years, a growing number of athletes are choosing early specialization such that they limit their participation to only one sport even before reaching high school (Wojtys 2013). The growing number of travel leagues for young athletes (seven to eight years of age) and the increasing number of sports boarding schools also contribute to larger numbers of athletes specializing early.

....

KEY POINT *Evidence of Increasing Early Specialization*

- 77% of high school athletic directors report an increasing trend in specialization.
- 70% of United States Tennis Association junior tennis players specialized at an average age of 10.4 years.

....

Why Early Specialization?

One of the first questions to consider when weighing the arguments regarding specialization versus diversification is what the goals are for the athlete. If the goals for the athlete revolve around sports enjoyment, physical activity participation, character development, learning to commit to practice and be competitive, and social opportunities, then it is hard to develop a strong argument for early specialization. Playing multiple sports, on the other hand, gives athletes opportunities to achieve these goals while also allowing them to self-select the most enjoyable activities for them. Furthermore, by having a broad repertoire of sports competencies, multisport athletes are more likely to remain active into adulthood. So, what types of goals for athletes would lead to a need for early specialization? Early specialization becomes relevant when athletes (with the support of their parents and coaches) want to pursue elite-level performance and believe that this is the correct path to that goal. So, the question we need to ask is, does early specialization or sports diversification produce a higher likelihood of competing at an elite level? There are several answers to consider, but let's start by examining the differences between elite-level performers and non-elite performers. In general, because movements have become automatic for elite athletes and because of their expertise, they have reached a level of performance that is clearly different from what we see in more novice performers.

KEY POINT *Elite Athletes Compared with Novice Athletes*

Elite athletes

- have more automatic movements,
- look like they are using less effort when they perform,
- have more automatic movement patterns, making them more consistent and more flexible in their responses,
- have superior perceptions of body position,
- have superior self-monitoring skills so they can analyze their movements and make corrections, and
- are quicker and more accurate in terms of pattern recognition so they can identify important elements or moments in the game at a glance.

(*Source*: Abernethy, Burgess-Limerick, and Parks 1994)

....

Is Early Specialization Necessary or Sufficient to Reach Elite Levels of Performance?

One way that experts have determined when an athlete needs to specialize is to look at the ages at which athletes achieve top performances in various sports. Studies have been done across a wide range of sports with evidence showing that in power-based events, peak performance occurs dramatically earlier than in sports that require aerobic endurance. Let's look at a few average ages of peak performance by sport (Allen and Hopkins 2015):

- Power-based events
  - *Throwing events (1–5 seconds): ~27 years*
  - *Swimming events (21–245 seconds): ~20 years*
- Endurance events
  - *Swimming events (2–15 minutes): ~20 years*
  - *Ultradistance cycling (27–29 hours): ~39 years*
- Mixed events
  - *Ice hockey: ~28 years*
  - *Tennis: ~23 years*
  - *Golf: ~33 years*

These numbers indicate that in these sports, peak performance occurs in adulthood. When peak performance is observed in adulthood, experts agree that there is no need to specialize until adolescence. In support of this argument, a survey of NCAA Division I female athletes found that only 17 percent had limited their participation to one sport prior to entering college. In other words, 83 percent were playing more than one sport throughout their high school years and still achieved elite status by playing at a Division I level (Malina 2010). Thus, high levels of performance can be achieved in these sports with specializing held off until late adolescence.

There are some sports, however, in which peak performance occurs at a much younger age. These are sports such as gymnastics, rhythmic gymnastics, figure skating, and diving, where there is a biomechanical advantage to competing prior to reaching full maturational size. So, the question then likely comes back to what the goals are for the athlete. If the athlete is a gymnast, a figure skater, or a diver and his or her goal is to compete at an Olympic level, then evidence supports the need to start focusing exclusively on a single sport at an earlier age. However, only an incredibly small number of athletes will achieve success at an Olympic level. If the goal is to compete collegiately, remember that the chances of this are also small, particularly for these sports.

....

KEY POINT *Limited Opportunities at the College Level for Gymnastics and Figure Skating*

Sport	Opportunities
Gymnastics	14 men's and 62 women's NCAA Division I teams
Figure skating	61 universities with club programs; 4 programs with full or close to full scholarships (accommodating 81–104 athletes)

....

In fact, early specialization does not result in large percentages of athletes reaching high levels of success. In countries where early sports specialization happens at a national level through sports schools, only a very small percentage of athletes identified at a young age for their talents are actually successful at elite levels. Thus, the vast majority of children who choose early sports specialization and commit to deliberate practice of only one sport for years will *not* be successful at an elite level.

....

KEY POINT *Evidence against Early Specialization*

- Of 35,000 Russian athletes training at sports schools from a young age, only 0.14 percent advanced to an elite level of performance.
- In a seven-year follow-up of top youth athletes selected at an early age, only 1.7% earned a medal at an international championship.

....

The 10,000 Hours Rule

Have you heard of the 10,000 hours rule? This "rule" has been used to support arguments for early specialization in sport. The 10,000 hours rule says that the attainment of elite status in sports relies on the acquisition of ten years or 10,000 hours of practice. This proposal has been further refined to suggest that 10,000 hours of *deliberate* practice are required where deliberate practice is defined as practice with a purpose that is effortful and not necessarily enjoyable. The evidence supporting this amount of time being critical for the attainment of elite status initially came from research with musicians. Thus, the extent to which it applies to sports is unclear. In fact, many experts would argue that 10,000 hours is neither necessary nor sufficient for elite sports performance. Let's look at what we know.

First, there is not a causative relationship between 10,000 hours of deliberate practice and the attainment of elite-level status. That is, I can't just choose a young athlete at random, expose the athlete to 10,000 hours of deliberate practice, and have a guarantee that the athlete will be able to compete at an elite level—there are simply too many other factors that come into play. In addition, there are elite-level athletes who report that the amount of deliberate practice that they have devoted specifically to one sport ranges from as few as 600 hours to 6,026 hours—not even close to 10,000 hours (Baker, Côté, and Abernethy 2003).

Second, participation in multiple sports contributes to performance in a single sport once specialization occurs. This is because of the positive transfer of foundational motor skills and of tactical decision-making across sports. For example, think about how similar throwing a baseball, softball, or football and hitting a tennis ball or volleyball serve are from a motor performance perspective. Consider the similarities between the offensive and defensive strategies of basketball, soccer, field hockey, ice hockey, and lacrosse. In my experience, the best soccer goalkeepers I've ever played with were also softball shortstops and basketball players. If you think of many elite athletes today, most of them played multiple sports. Noted professional basketball players LeBron James and Michael Jordan played more than one sport in high school—LeBron played football and basketball and Michael played basketball, baseball, and football. Alex Morgan, one of the top women's soccer players in the world, played softball, soccer, and basketball until she was fourteen years old (All White Kit 2011). Annika Sörenstam, one of the greatest women golfers of all time, played tennis and soccer and was a talented skier before picking up golf as a twelve-year-old. Wayne Gretzky was involved in multiple sports and played hockey only in the winter months. Plenty of elite athletes did not specialize early, and the evidence does not support the 10,000 hours rule as a rationale to support early specialization.

Risks of Early Specialization

In addition to arguing against the need for early specialization from the basis of the age of achieving peak performance, there are three additional arguments against early specialization and for sports diversification. First, athletes who specialize early with the concomitant focus on deliberate practice have a heightened risk of burnout (see chapter 8). Second, early specialization is associated with a greater risk of overuse injuries. This is particularly true in the sport of baseball, where increases in Tommy John surgeries (surgeries to the ulnar collateral ligament to repair overuse injuries) have been linked to early specialization (Mautner and Blazuk 2015; Pennington 2005). Third, early specialization restricts athletes' exposure to a variety of sports, which is linked to lower levels of enjoyment and a lesser likelihood that they will remain physically active into adulthood.

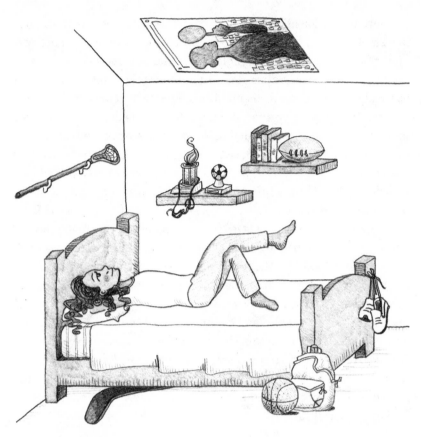

Participation in multiple sports is the right choice for all athletes—from those who enjoy participating at a recreational level to those with aspirations of playing in college or at higher levels. *Illustration by Dominy Alderman.*

Recommendations

Based upon the evidence, you should encourage your athletes to participate in multiple sports rather than limit themselves to one sport early on. Children five to twelve years old should participate in a wide range of different sports. This will allow them to develop movement skills and strategies that will generalize across sports and enhance performance across activities. Children thirteen to fifteen years old may begin to restrict their participation to fewer activities. This is a natural response to increasing levels of school and extracurricular commitments but also likely reflects children starting to choose the activities they most enjoy. Children who are over sixteen may choose to commit to a single sport if a high level of performance in this sport is their priority. Staying diverse is also perfectly appropriate and has its own benefits, but specializing at this time may make sense for athletes with aspirations of making valuable contributions to their high school teams or playing at a higher level.

In addition, experts argue that for the development of sports expertise, athletes need to participate in a variety of sports activities that include and progress through stages of free play, deliberate play, structured practice, and deliberate practice. The idea here is that the relative focus of athletes' activities should progress through these levels of involvement in a way that reflects their stage of development. In other words, an early focus on deliberate practice is not appropriate for young athletes, who should be engaged in more free and deliberate play.

· ·

KEY POINT *Different Forms of Play/Practice*

- Free play: completely unrestricted play that isn't reliant on any existing rules
- Deliberate play: a set of implicit or explicit rules govern the activity, but the primary goal is enjoyment of the activity
- Structured practice: more typical of organized sports with a goal of improving performance
- Deliberate practice: highly structured, requires high levels of effort, is not necessarily enjoyable, and is specifically designed to improve performance

(*Source*: Côté and Hay 2002; Côté 1999)

· ·

Finally, there is substantial evidence that sports diversification has benefits that are not seen in those who specialize early. Sports diversification is more likely to lead to success in sports, and there is evidence that elite athletes actually were more likely to begin intense training later than those who made it to near-elite levels (Jayanthi et al. 2013). This may be because participation in multiple sports allows for a transfer of skills that results in the need for less sport-specific deliberate practice to achieve expertise (Côté, Baker, and Abernethy 2003). In addition, and importantly, diversification results in higher levels of enjoyment, the likelihood of longer participation in sport, less likelihood of burnout and overuse injuries, and opportunities to become competent in a variety of sports, which provide more choices for physical activity participation in adulthood. All of this evidence indicates that even athletes who have goals of elite-level performance are most likely to reach these goals through diversification.

....

KEY QUOTE *Even Elite Athletes Argue against Early Specialization*

I played everything. I played lacrosse, baseball, hockey, soccer, track and field. I was a big believer that you played hockey in the winter and when the season was over you hung up your skates and you played something else.

WAYNE GRETZKY

....

Why This Matters

Although the commitment of a vast number of hours of practice and competition is necessary to attain elite levels of performance in sport, the evidence does not support that early specialization or 10,000 hours of participation are either necessary or sufficient. In fact, early specialization increases the likelihood of burnout and overuse injuries and minimizes athletes' ability to stay active into adulthood. By contrast, participation in multiple sports allows for transfer of skills, higher levels of enjoyment, less risk of burnout, greater opportunity to attain a high level of performance, and greater likelihood of remaining physically active as an adult. Furthermore, think back to the mission statements of sports organizations and the goals of most parents in terms of their children's sports participation. Diversification meets the goals focused on character development, on learning to work hard and persist, and on honing skills that will contribute to success as an adult, without the downside of specialization.

Activity

1. Consider your own sports background. What sports did you play growing up? Identify aspects of one sport that contributed to your ability to play another sport. Now think about the sport you are coaching. What sports could your athletes participate in that would provide the most transfer to the sport you're coaching? Are your athletes playing those sports?

2. You may be faced with parents who are convinced that early specialization is the best path toward developing their young athlete. Write out what you might say to these parents to convince them that diversification is a better choice. Start with asking them to think about their goals for their child and then consider how the two approaches might help or hinder their child's ability to reach those goals.

CHAPTER ELEVEN

Practical Matters and Bringing It All Together

Let's consider some practical applications for the ideas I've presented. Let me start by reminding you of one thing—the reason you are coaching. You are coaching for the love of the game. You are coaching so that the athletes you are working with come to your practices excited to be there, so that they tell their friends about how much fun they are having in their sport, and so that they have a sense of accomplishment and feelings of mastery when they play. You are coaching to help athletes develop positive characteristics that will stay with them in sports and beyond. If you can keep these ideas at the forefront of your mind throughout the season, you will be taking a key step toward being a great coach.

Playing Time

Playing time is a topic that is critically important from the perspective of the athletes. Prior to a game, ask the players on your team how much of the game they'd like to play, and you will find that most of them would like to play the entire game. But typically they can't all play the entire time because, if you're lucky, you are coaching a team that has at least a few more players than are necessary. This means that you will be faced with the challenge of working out substitutions. A key question to consider and actually plan out in advance of the game is how you intend to run your subs. If you are coaching a team with which you can take a developmental approach (that is, every team with athletes younger than fourteen and many teams with players who are fourteen to fifteen), then you should make every effort possible to ensure that playing time is roughly equal across players. If player development is the primary goal for you as the coach, for the league, and for the players, then there is no further decision-making necessary; there is merely the matter of giving your athletes equal time at play.

When giving athletes equal time at play, you should consider several points. First, you should be doing everything possible to ensure that all of your players have a good experience in the competition. That means that you do not want to put players in a position where they are likely to fail in a very public way. In other words, you should not put your weakest athlete in as goalkeeper, as the first server in a volleyball set, or as the point guard in basketball. These positions by their very nature put the player in a position where a poor performance will be a very public experience that may have big ramifications for the entire team. Rather, you should be very tactical in putting your weaker players in. Put them in positions where they can play with confidence. Make sure that they are joined by stronger players who can help provide support. Start them out in positions that are not central to the play (for example, outfielder in baseball/softball; outside forward/attacker/defender in soccer, lacrosse, field hockey, ice hockey). In fact, if you are competing against a team that also has weaker players, you could discretely arrange with the other coach to agree to put your weaker players in at the same time to attempt to keep the competition level as even as possible.

Second, you should be sure that your athletes have had opportunities in practice to play all positions and that you have prepared them appropriately for the positions in which they might initially find themselves in competition. This will help them acquire the necessary confidence and experience to be able to do their best. No athlete wants to compete in a position, situation, or role for which he or she has not prepared.

Third, offer your support and encouragement equally to all players and regardless of outcome. Your focus should be 100 percent on effort and persistence. You should work hard to avoid looking disappointed or frustrated with player performance. Instead, be encouraging and positive by verbally and nonverbally rewarding players who are working hard, who are following your instructions and training, and who are doing the best they can. Remember that if you can get all the players on your team to give their best in the game, then you will help your team rise to its potential.

Fourth, if you are making substitutions that are not based upon a particular time point in a game, try not to substitute someone out just after he or she has made a mistake. If you can, wait a few minutes to allow the athlete some additional playing opportunities, which will help to emphasize that you weren't substituting him or her out (that is, punishing the athlete) for the mistake. If you do need to substitute a player out right away, be sure to explain to him or her the reason why and to also talk through how he or she might improve next time so as not to repeat the mistake.

As an example of what not to do, I was recently watching a girls' middle school volleyball game. The teams played two sets that ended 25–12 and 26–14. In total, then, the teams played almost 80 points. In watching them play, I immediately noticed that there were two athletes on the bench. In this particular competition, one of these players came into one set for six points and the other came into one set for three points. So, these two players essentially got to play for 8 percent and 4 percent of the competition, respectively. How do you think those two felt after that event? Certainly, they could not have had much fun, they could not feel proud of their efforts, and they could not really even feel as if they were contributors to the team. How are they supposed to improve their ability to perform in competitive settings? Not giving these players equal playing time is such a disservice to them and really to the whole team. The whole team is hearing the message loud and clear that the only thing that matters is winning and that there is not a commitment to developing individual players. Remember at the developmental level, players should get roughly equivalent playing time because the outcome really doesn't matter. Your goal is to help all of the players improve as much as possible, which necessitates that they have ample opportunities to compete.

Attitude

I must emphasize how important it is that you demonstrate to the athletes your love for the game. Think back to chapter 1, when you listed the reasons why you wanted to be a coach and saw that they all relate to love—love of the game, love of the athletes, and a desire to help the athletes develop love for the sport. So, share that love with the athletes. Be fun! Be positive! Joke with the team. Too many coaches seem to walk onto the field and suddenly feel that they have to be an authoritarian

By following the guidance provided in this book, you will have a positive influence on your athletes: you will help them maintain their love of the game, reach their potential in sports and beyond, and develop as young people. *Illustration by Dominy Alderman.*

overseer who keeps the athletes on task at all expense, denigrates the athletes when they lose their focus or don't perform well, and takes all the fun out of the sport. Don't be that coach! If the athletes are not having fun at your practice, then in my opinion you have already failed, and nothing else that you might accomplish will change that. Having fun and working hard are not opposites; they are perfectly compatible. The athletes come to you wanting to learn, to improve, and to have fun. So, teach them the game while incorporating fun and a positive attitude into every practice. I recently got to observe a fantastic swim coach who motivated her players through her own enthusiasm. Prior to a meet, the swimmers got together in one corner of the pool to do their team cheer. This was not a simple or short cheer; this was a long, complex cheer that involved a back-and-forth between coach and athletes, lots of splashing and smacking of the water for noise, and a growing level of volume until it reached a fever pitch. The watching teams literally stood and gave the team a standing ovation in response. What a fantastic way to get the athletes excited about their upcoming opportunity to compete!

By contrast, sometimes I think that coaches have watched too many sports movies. They appear to be trying to emulate behaviors of movie coaches who all seem to go through very similar scripts. In the movies, the team is struggling either because the athletes are not very good or because they have faced some adversity. A hard-nosed coach comes in, works the players hard, and verbally or physically abuses them but ultimately molds them into a cohesive unit. In the end, the players come together to perform well, recognize that the coach has a softer side, and win a state championship (*Hoosiers*, *Remember the Titans*, *Miracle Season*) or a national (*Glory Road*, *The Mighty Macs*) or international title (*Miracle*). As examples of such "inspiration," I've heard youth coaches say that to help their athletes recognize the value of communicating during a game, they're going to prohibit talking during practice. I've seen youth coaches have athletes run suicides after a loss, tell players they need to run laps until they can focus better during practice, and sit players out of games for not performing well. None of this is consistent with the goals of developing young athletes so that they can reach their potential. In fact, if it weren't hurting the young athletes so much, these behaviors would be laughable because they are in such contrast to the goals of youth sport. Remember that you are in charge of the practice, and so the extent to which athletes invest themselves in your training is going to be reflective of how much you give them! Give them joy, give them fun, give them confidence, give them opportunities to participate, give them chances for success, and give them respect. If you do those things, then your athletes will commit to training, they will improve, and they will give you an opportunity to achieve success even when defined in terms of outcome. Then you will find that coaching can be one of the most rewarding experiences you can possibly have.

Final words of Advice

I end this chapter by providing some advice offered by the young athletes themselves. The first is from an eleven-year-old boy who has played soccer for five years and who has had the chance to play for many different coaches who range in their ability to "reach" the athletes. I asked him to tell me what things a coach does that influence the extent to which a practice is fun or not fun. These points (see table 11.1) are quite simple, and if you put yourself in the position of the athlete, I'm sure you will recognize their wisdom. You will notice that most of these points revolve around the specifics of designing a practice.

Next, I asked a thirteen-year-old girl who is currently playing middle school volleyball what she thought coaches needed to remember to help keep practices fun. Her points (see table 11.2) were much more about the feedback offered from the coaches than about the nuts-and-bolts of a practice, but the message is somewhat the same.

Table 11.1. Advice for coaches from an eleven-year-old soccer player

Do	Don't
Give effective demonstrations with clear instructions.	Explain things for too long.
Give the athletes feedback by pulling them out to tell them what you would like to see and then get them back into the game.	Use benching as a punishment.
Switch people around so they can learn all the positions.	Put people in positions that never change (offense/defense, setter, pitcher).
Use multiple lines so athletes get to participate more.	Use a single line for activities.
Make the teams as even as possible and adjust if necessary.	Leave teams uneven in a scrimmage.
Make practice fun by changing activities quickly, keeping everyone involved, and being brief in making your coaching points.	Make practice boring by keeping athletes in an activity too long, explaining for too long, or limiting participation.
Include variety and think about fun activities instead of thinking about them as drills.	Do the same thing at every practice.

So, with the perspectives of the young athletes in mind and recalling why you started coaching in the first place, I encourage you to also remember the following:

- Fun is the top priority—keep them engaged, keep it playful, keep it fun.
- Every child is different—your job is to meet all the kids where they are.
- Children want to play—keep playing time as even as possible during practices and competitions.
- Children will do what you reinforce—reward effort and persistence.
- Children want to get better—design your practices with a specific objective and build your activities around that objective.

- Everyone can be a winner when the focus is on self-improvement.
- Children are playing to have fun—I can't repeat this enough. The minute it's not fun, that's the first minute toward that child making the decision to drop out.

....

Table 11.2. Advice for coaches from a thirteen-year-old volleyball player

Do	Don't
Focus on improvement and effort.	Focus on outcome.
Offer shout-outs to individual players for things they did well (and make sure everyone gets one of these every few practices or games).	Ignore players when they do well.
Ask the athletes what they would like to do as a fun activity and what they think they need to work on.	Have boring practices.
Give players pointers and then give them a chance to work on those before telling them they didn't do what you asked.	Try to be so inspirational that you sound like a broken record.
Recognize that athletes might do better in practice than in games because they haven't repeated the skills enough to be proficient in more challenging situations.	Expect players to be perfect in games.
Tell players what to do.	Tell players what NOT to do.
Identify places where players can improve and teach them how to improve.	Tell athletes they're not giving enough effort when they are trying their hardest.

....

I trust that you're coaching for the right reasons, and I know you can have a powerful, positive impact on the children. By keeping your focus on the love of the game, you can ensure that your athletes have a great season. If the athletes have fun and improve, you and the athletes will all be WINNERS, and your athletes will develop their own LOVE OF THE GAME!

CHAPTER TWELVE

....

For Organizations, Athletic Departments, and Officials

....

As a final chapter, I want to include some thoughts and recommendations for those of you who are contributing to the youth sports experience through your role as an administrator of an organization or athletic department or as a youth sports official.

Administrators

As a coach, you might have the opportunity to interact with administrators so that you can advocate for the ideas found in this book. And if you coach for long enough, you may one day end up in an administrative position that will allow you to have a broad impact on the youth sports experience. My recommendations for administrators are motivated by the same ideas I have expressed throughout this book and boil down to the fact that your number one priority should be the experience of the athletes. If you are currently an administrator, I hope you will consider some of these ideas right away to enhance your organization's positive impact on youth athletes.

My first recommendation is that meetings, education, and resources be provided for the coaches in your organization to make sure that the coaches are creating a positive environment that fosters the development of youth athletes. The meetings can be used to talk about the mission of the organization, to provide an opportunity for coaches to meet one another, and to deliver information about education and resources available to the coaches. By providing education and resources, organizations can help ensure that their coaches are well versed in coaching pedagogy, in developmental considerations for youth athletes, and in league rules and policies. Those of you in administration should also encourage your coaches to pursue educational opportunities relevant to the sport and, whenever possible, provide financial support to facilitate these occasions. These educational resources might be offered by the organization or advertised when they are available locally, regionally, or online. In addition, organizations should develop mentoring programs through which experienced, positive coaches make themselves available as resources to less-experienced coaches or to those who have room to improve in terms of how they work with their athletes. If a coach is motivated to do the best job possible, then that coach should be open to learning from others. It would be fantastic to see clubs/organizations/schools really taking advantage of the great coaches they have to help their less-experienced coaches improve. Related to this, organizations should provide curricula for their coaches to ensure that the youth sports experience is consistently positive, developmentally appropriate, and designed to advance the skills sets of the athletes.

An additional support that I encourage you to provide to your coaches is to give them feedback on what they are doing. Our teachers in the schools regularly receive peer evaluations of their teaching, which gives them critical information to improve their skills. But very few sports organizations include this as a part of their system, even though this is a great way for coaches to learn how to get better at what they are doing. If experienced coaches are able to provide professional, critical feedback, all coaches can improve in their craft. Such feedback also provides a level of accountability to coaches because they know that they may be evaluated at any time.

Another important recommendation is that leagues and sports organizations carefully consider the rules that govern their sports. Of course, the top priority is to keep the sport safe for the athletes. This is evidenced by rules enacted by the United States Youth Soccer Association that restrict heading by soccer athletes who are twelve and younger, by recommendations that children not play tackle football until they are fourteen years of age (Farrey and Solomon 2018), by USA Hockey and Hockey Canada not allowing checking by players under fifteen years of age, and by leagues such as Little League Baseball and the Amateur Softball Association where coaches serve as pitchers for younger players.

But leagues would also benefit from rules that help keep children safe psychologically; that is, those that help minimize the likelihood of extremely lopsided competitions that can have a negative impact on the athletes' experiences. So, if you are an administrator for a league, organization, or conference that involves youth athletes fourteen and under, consider what you might to do reduce the likelihood of a lopsided outcome.

There are two reasons why preventing a lopsided outcome is important. First, if one team is being crushed by another, emotionally it can be very upsetting. The competition is definitely not fun for the losing team. But what about the team that is doing the crushing? Its players are probably not having that much fun, either, because of the lack of challenge. Remember that youth athletes recognize that winning is fun only when they're playing against equal competition. Second, when competitions are extremely lopsided, neither team benefits from the competition itself—neither team's players' performance improves. The winning team is not challenged, and so its athletes' level of play can drop, while those on the losing team do not have enough opportunity to even try to play the game. My advice is thus to modify the rules to minimize lopsided outcomes. I know that probably sounds like sacrilege to some of you, but there is nothing sacred about the rules! If you are truly making the needs of the athletes the top priority in youth sport, then don't be afraid to modify the rules of the game.

What kind of rules are we talking about? I have heard them euphemistically referred to as "mercy rules," and I think they are probably well intended. But we need to think carefully about whether these rules are actually "merciful." In a middle school girls' soccer league, I recently learned of a mercy rule that says that if one team gets ahead by ten goals, the game is stopped. I'm not sure how that is actually merciful. Remember, this is middle school soccer. Why should the score ever get to be 10–0? Who could possibly support one team running up a score like that against another team? And how does it help either team if the game is stopped? Talk about embarrassing for the losing team! And then none of the athletes get to play at all.

So, what about some different adjustments that could be made to make the game more competitive? What if when one team got ahead by four goals, the coach pulled a player off the field and played with ten instead of eleven? This might be a great solution if the winning team doesn't have too many players sitting on the bench; if there are, then this isn't such a great idea because it means fewer athletes are getting

Administrators, league officials, and coaches should be willing to modify the rules or to make any necessary adjustments to keep the competition even so that all athletes benefit from the opportunity to compete.
Illustration by Dominy Alderman.

the opportunity to play. In that situation, maybe once the team is ahead by four goals, the coach could make four substitutions of weaker players for stronger players. If the team scores again, the coach could then substitute out two more of the stronger players for weaker players. Obviously, this could continue until the winning team had completely replaced the team on the field with weaker players. Another idea is for the coach of the winning team to require his or her athletes to play the ball back to the goalkeeper every time they gain possession from the other team. If they didn't play it back, any goal scored wouldn't count (officials could just call the goal back as they do when an offside call is made).

This requirement would be great for the dominant team because it would force players to learn how to play possession, it would slow the game down in terms of scoring by the winning team, and it would give the weaker team a chance to regroup and organize its defense.

I have seen similar lopsided competitions in volleyball. The overhand serve is a very powerful weapon in middle school volleyball. And when teams have a good server, they can go on extremely long scoring runs. This is so painful to watch because the receiving team doesn't even get to rotate. So, the server can just keep serving to the same players who demonstrate repeatedly that they are unable to get the ball back. Talk about demoralizing! How about a rule that says that no player can serve more than five times before it's a side-out? Since points are currently scored in volleyball for side-outs, this might have to necessitate a rule change where in this situation, the team that is serving merely gives up the serve to the other team and no point is awarded. Another way to adjust for this kind of a run of points would be to allow the receiving team to rotate. That again requires either a rule change or the cooperation of the official to allow that to happen. Another adjustment that wouldn't require a rule change would be for the coach—who recognizes that there is no reason to allow his or her team to run up the score—to instruct the server to switch to an underhanded serve. Any of these adjustments would allow the receiving team to have a chance to get the ball back, which would benefit both teams.

In summary, I strongly encourage administrators to help get a handle on lopsided scoring. If you've been to many competitions of athletes who are under fourteen, you probably have noticed that the scores are often uneven. Rather than stopping competitions if the scores get completely out of control, leagues should adopt rules that help keep competition even. If administrators won't make these changes, then I encourage coaches to be sensitive to this situation. If you are coaching the winning team, your athletes are not benefiting from a lopsided score. Use all of your creative energy to figure out how to adjust what is happening to make the match or game more competitive. If you are coaching the losing team, then obviously you would appreciate these adjustments made by the coach of the winning team as they would allow your players a chance to improve while also maintaining their dignity. Remember, this is a win for both teams!

Relatedly, if you are an administrator or have control over your schedule, I want to make a plea for a focus more on practices than on games. In a recent middle school soccer season, the team had only four practices scheduled before the first game. The players then had three games and one practice every week for the first three weeks, two games and one practice each week for the next two weeks, two games and two practices for a week, and then three games and one practice in the week prior to the conference tournament. That adds up to eighteen games and only twelve practices in their nine-week soccer season! There are a couple of problems with this. First, this is middle school soccer, which should by definition be a time to develop players. Coaches cannot possibly develop their players when they have so few practices and so many competitions. Second, this is a huge physical load on these young athletes and students. Remember too that we are talking about this high number of games for athletes who are not physically mature. Although I have not seen published guidelines or recommendations for limiting the number of games for youth athletes, participating in such a high number of games makes no sense because it places young athletes at an increased risk for injury and clearly does not focus on development. At least in this case, there was typically only one practice per week. By comparison, although college soccer teams practice much more than middle school teams, they participate in approximately the same number of games over the course of a twelve-week season. And, at the adult level, considerations are given to the number of games played relative to the days of rest in between with a goal of not putting the athletes at a heightened risk of injury.

Officials

The last comment I want to make is for officials. Officials have a huge amount of control over the experience of the youth athletes in a competition. Paying attention, making assertive calls, being consistent in your interpretation and implementation of the rules, and clearly communicating your decisions go a long way to keeping coaches, parents, and athletes focused on the game rather than on you. I encourage officials to give 100 percent, even when officiating at youth sporting events at the lower levels of competition. Ask yourself why you are officiating. If you are officiating in a sport, I imagine this is a reflection of your love of the game. If you love the game, then do everything in your power to make sure that the participants have a positive experience. Your primary job is to make sure the players follow the rules of the game. To do this, you must remain focused, demonstrate enthusiasm, and communicate clearly. But an official's secondary job is to ensure that your influence contributes to the athletes' positive experience. If you are officiating in youth sports, then I strongly encourage you to tailor the way you officiate based upon the age group you are working with, the score, and the level of competition.

The best officials I've seen are able to adapt their style of officiating to the age group they are working with. When working with the youngest athletes, the officials make a call and then briefly explain that call to the players. They help the players understand where to line up and what to do in the event of a dead ball. They give warnings instead of stopping play when they need to correct an athlete's behavior. And they interact with parents and coaches in positive and respectful ways. The best officials also adjust their behavior to the level of competition and the score. Some officials recognize that if a team is losing 0–4 in a sport like soccer, field hockey, or lacrosse, or 22–4 in basketball, there is no need to call a minor foul on the team that is behind. That foul can be let go so that play can continue and the team that is behind can have an opportunity to compete in that moment. Again, a word of warning to the athlete who fouls will likely suffice, since the team that is ahead doesn't need additional opportunities to score. I'm not suggesting that you ignore egregious offenses, rather that you adjust the strictness of your officiating based upon these important variables. If you are able to do so successfully, you will contribute positively to the youth athletes' experience.

I end by reiterating that if you are a coach, an official, or an administrator in youth sports and if you have read this book, then clearly you must love the game! Please do everything in your power to ensure that the athletes you interact with develop this same love of the game as they participate in youth sports and as they develop as individuals.

ACKNOWLEDGMENTS

....

I would like to acknowledge Paige Wagner, Liz Etnier, and Shelley Etnier for their input on initial drafts of this book. In addition, I thank my partner, Paige, for providing me with unwavering support throughout this process—despite that preparing the final stages of the book occasionally took me away from family time. I sincerely thank Dominy Alderman for providing her wonderful illustrations for this book! She masterfully captures the sentiments of the chapters and artfully conveys the emotions of the athletes. I would also like to acknowledge Jay Miller and Tony Amorose for their comments and suggestions on the final draft of the book. I have such admiration for Jay as a coach and teacher and for Tony as an academic and researcher, and I feel fortunate to have benefited from their input. Finally, I thank Lucas Church, Julie Bush, Mary Caviness, and the other staff from the University of North Carolina Press for seeing value in my work and for assisting me through the publication process.

This book would not have been written if it weren't for the youth sports experiences my partner and I have had with our children, Payton, James, and Max. We recognize that as parents we have one primary responsibility, and that is to nurture and safeguard our children's personal growth so that they can explore their passions, develop their strengths, improve in areas of weakness, and learn to display compassion. It has been a joy for us to watch our children grow in all of these ways. I recognize that youth sports participation is a setting in which my children and other children have the opportunity to pursue these goals, and I am committed to helping improve the youth sports experience for all.

This book is also a result of the early introduction to sports that I had because of my parents, David and Liz Etnier. They gave me copious opportunities to participate in youth sports as a child and, ultimately, set me on a path to pursue a career in the area of sport and exercise psychology.

RESOURCES

....

YOUTH SPORTS ORGANIZATIONS PROMOTING POSITIVE YOUTH SPORTS EXPERIENCES

- Aspen Institute Project Play, https://www.aspenprojectplay .org/
- Center for the Study of Sport in Society, https://www .northeastern.edu/sportinsociety/
- Inside Out Initiative, https://insideoutinitiative.org/
- National Alliance for Youth Sports, https://www.nays.org/ resources/nays-documents/national-standards-for-youth -sports/
- National Council of Youth Sports, https://www.ncys.org/
- North American Youth Sport Institute, http://www.naysi.com/
- Positive Coaching Alliance, https://www.positivecoach.org/

ORGANIZATIONS, CENTERS, AND INSTITUTES CONDUCTING RESEARCH ON YOUTH SPORTS

- Institute for the Study of Youth Sports, https://edwp.educ.msu .edu/isys/
- Tucker Center for Research on Girls and Women in Sport, https://edwp.educ.msu.edu/isys/

SITES OFFERING FREE CONCUSSION TRAINING

- Centers for Disease Control concussion training for coaches, https://www.cdc.gov/headsup/youthsports/training/index .html
- National Alliance for Youth Sports, https://www.nays.org/ additional-training/preview/concussion-training.cfm

REFERENCES

....

Abernethy, B., R. Burgess-Limerick, and S. Parks. 1994. "Contrasting Approaches to the Study of Motor Expertise." *Quest* 46, no. 2: 186–98.

Allen, S. V., and W. G. Hopkins. 2015. "Age of Peak Competitive Performance of Elite Athletes: A Systematic Review." *Sports Medicine* 45, no. 10: 1431–41. doi: 10.1007/s40279–015–0354–3.

All White Kit. 2011. "20 Questions with Alex Morgan." All White Kit, April 1. http://www.allwhitekit.com/?p=5469.

Amorose, A. J., and D. Anderson-Butcher. 2007. "Autonomy-Supportive Coaching and Self-Determined Motivation in High School and College Athletes: A Test of Self-Determination Theory." *Psychology of Sport and Exercise* 8, no. 5 (September) : 654–70.

Amorose, A. J., and T. S. Horn. 2000. "Intrinsic Motivation: Relationships with Collegiate Athletes' Gender, Scholarship Status, and Perceptions of Their Coaches Behavior." *Journal of Sport Exercise Psychology* 22, no. 1: 63–84.

Archer, J. 2004. "Sex Differences in Aggression in Real-World Settings: A Meta-Analytic Review." *Review of General Psychology* 8, no. 4: 291–322.

Armstrong, N., G. Tomkinson, and U. Ekelund. 2011. "Aerobic Fitness and Its Relationship to Sport, Exercise Training and Habitual Physical Activity during Youth." *British Journal of Sports Medicine* 45, no. 11: 849–58.

Babkes, M. L., and M. R. Weiss. 1999. "Parental Influence on Children's Cognitive and Affective Responses to Competitive Soccer Participation." *Pediatric Exercise Science* 11, no. 1: 44–62.

Bacon, J. U. 2016. "To Get a College Scholarship: Forget the Field, Hit the Books." Accessed June 20, 2019. https://www.npr.org/2016/11/16/502274825 /forget-the-fields-hit-the-books-to-get-a-college-scholarship.

Baillargeon, R. H., M. Zoccolillo, K. Keenan, S. Cote, D. Perusse, H. X. Wu, M. Boivin, and R. E. Tremblay. 2007. "Gender Differences in Physical Aggression: A Prospective Population-Based Survey of Children before and after 2 Years of Age." *Developmental Psychology* 43, no. 1: 13–26. doi: 10.1037/0012–1649.43.1.13.

Baker, J., J. Côté, and B. Abernethy. 2003. "Sport-Specific Practice and the Development of Expert Decision-Making in Team Ball Sports." *Journal of Applied Sport Psychology* 15, no. 1: 12–25.

Baquet, G., E. van Praagh, and S. Berthoin. 2003. "Endurance Training and Aerobic Fitness in Young People." *Sports Medicine* 33, no. 15: 1127–43.

Bisi, M. C., and R. Stagni. 2016. "Development of Gait Motor Control: What Happens after a Sudden Increase in Height during Adolescence?" *Biomedical Engineering Online* 15, no. 1: 47. doi: 10.1186/s12938–016–0159–0.

Columbus Dispatch. 2010. "Children May Be Vulnerable in $5 Billion Youth-Sports Industry." August 29. http://www.dispatch.com/content/ stories/local/2010/08/29/children-may-be-vulnerable-in-5-billion-youth -sports-industry.html.

Côté, J., J. Baker, and B. Abernethy. 2003. "From Play to Practice: A Developmental Framework for the Acquisition of Expertise in Team Sport." In *Expert Performance in Sports: Advances in Research on Sport Expertise*, edited by J. Starkes and K. A. Ericsson, 89–113. Urbana, Ill.: Human Kinetics.

Côté, J., and J. Hay. 2002. "Children's Involvement in Sport: A Developmental Perspective." In *Psychological Foundations of Sport*, edited by J. M. Silva and D. E. Stevens, 484–502. Boston, Mass.: Allyn and Bacon.

DiFiori, J. P., H. J. Benjamin, J. S. Brenner, A. Gregory, N. Jayanthi, G. L. Landry, and A. Luke. 2014. "Overuse Injuries and Burnout in Youth Sports: A Position Statement from the American Medical Society for Sports Medicine." *British Journal of Sports Medicine* 48, no. 4: 287–88. doi: 10.1136/ bjsports-2013–093299.

Dorrance, A., and T. Nash. 1996. *Training Soccer Champions*. Brattleboro, Vt.: Echo Point Books and Media.

Dvorak, J., P. McCrory, and D. T. Kirkendall. 2007. "Head Injuries in the Female Football Player: Incidence, Mechanisms, Risk Factors and Management." *British Journal of Sports Medicine* 41, supp. 1: i44–i46. doi: 10.1136/ bjsm.2007.037960.

Dweck, C. 2016. *Mindset: The New Psychology of Success*. New York: Penguin Random House.

Eitzen, D. S., and G. H. Sage. 2009. *Sociology of North American Sport*. 8th ed. Boulder: Paradigm.

Engh, F. 2002. *Why Johnny Hates Sports*. Garden City Park, N.Y.: Square One Publishers.

Etnier, J. 2009. *Bring Your "A" Game: A Young Athlete's Guide to Mental Toughness*. Chapel Hill: University of North Carolina Press.

Farrey, T., and J. Solomon. 2018. "What If . . . Flag Becomes the Standard Way of Playing Football until High School?" In *Future of Sports*, edited by Aspen Institute, 1–27. Washington, D.C.: Aspen Institute.

Flanagan, L. 2017. "The Field Where Men Still Call the Shots: The Lack of Female Coaches in Youth Sports Can Make Lasting Impressions on Boys and Girls." *The Atlantic*, July 28. https://www.theatlantic.com/education/ archive/2017/07/the-field-where-men-still-call-the-shots/535167/.

Fry, M. D. 2000. "A Developmental Analysis of Children's and Adolescents' Understanding of Luck and Ability in the Physical Domain." *Journal of Sport and Exercise Psychology* 22: 145–66.

Gallahue, D. L., and J. C. Ozmun. 2006. *Understanding Motor Development: Infants, Children, Adolescents, Adults*. Boston: McGraw-Hill.

Gladwell, M. 2008. *Outliers: The Story of Success*. New York: Little, Brown.

Gneezy, U., and A. Rustichini. 2004. "Gender and Competition at a Young Age." *American Economic Review* 94, no. 2: 377–81.

Gould, D., and S. Carson. 2008. "Life Skills Development through Sport:

Current Status and Future Directions." *International Review of Sport and Exercise Psychology* 1, no. 1: 58–78.

Hardy, L. L., T. Reinten-Reynolds, P. Espinel, A. Zask, and A. D. Okely. 2012. "Prevalence and Correlates of Low Fundamental Movement Skill Competency in Children." *Pediatrics* 130, no. 2: e390–e398. doi: 10.1542/peds.2012-0345.

Hawkins, D., and J. Metheny. 2001. "Overuse Injuries in Youth Sports: Biomechanical Considerations." *Medicine and Science in Sports and Exercise* 33, no. 10: 1701–7.

Haywood, K., and N. Getchell. 2014. *Life Span Motor Development*. 6th ed. Urbana-Champaign, Ill.: Human Kinetics.

Hollembeak, J., and A. J. Amorose. 2005. "Perceived Coaching Behaviors and College Athletes' Intrinsic Motivation: A Test of Self-Determination Theory." *Journal of Applied Sport Psychology* 17: 20–36.

Hyde, J. S. 2014. "Gender Similarities and Differences." *Annual Review of Psychology* 65: 373–98. doi: 10.1146/annurev-psych-010213-115057.

Hyde, J. S., S. M. Lindberg, M. C. Linn, A. B. Ellis, and C. C. Williams. 2008. "Gender Similarities Characterize Math Performance." *Science* 321, no. 5888: 494–95. doi: 10.1126/science.1160364.

Iannelli, V. 2017. "The Importance of Free Play for Kids: Unstructured and Unscheduled Play Time." *Verywell Family*. Updated April 2, 2019. https://www.verywellfamily.com/the-importance-of-free-play-2633113.

Jayanthi, N., C. Pinkham, L. Dugas, B. Patrick, and C. Labella. 2013. "Sports Specialization in Young Athletes: Evidence-Based Recommendations." *Sports Health* 5, no. 3: 251–57. doi: 10.1177/1941738112464626.

Kelley, B., and C. Carchia. 2013. "Hey, Data Data—Swing!" *ESPN The Magazine*, July 11.

Kendall, B. 2018. "Rim Height and Ball Size: A Guide for Young Basketball Players." August 27. https://www.activekids.com/basketball/articles/rim-height-and-ball-size-a-guide-for-young-basketball-players.

LaVoi, N. M., E. Becker, and H. D. Maxwell. 2007. "'Coaching Girls': A Content Analysis of Best-Selling Popular Press Coaching Books." *Women in Sport and Physical Activity Journal* 16, no. 2: 7–20.

Lombardi, V., Jr. 2001. *What It Takes to Be #1: Vince Lombardi on Leadership*. New York: McGraw-Hill.

———. 2003. *The Lombardi Rules: 26 Lessons from Vince Lombardi—the World's Greatest Coach*. New York: McGraw-Hill.

Mageau, G. A., and R. J. Vallerand. 2003. "The Coach-Athlete Relationship: A Motivational Model." *Journal of Sports Sciences* 21, no. 11: 883–904. doi: 10.1080/0264041031000140374.

Malina, R. M. 2010. "Early Sport Specialization: Roots, Effectiveness, Risks." *Current Sports Medicine Reports* 9, no. 6: 364–71. doi: 10.1249/JSR.0b013e3181fe3166.

Malina, R. M., C. Bourchard, and O. Bar-Or. 2004. *Growth, Maturation, and Physical Activity*. Champaign, Ill.: Human Kinetics.

Martin, S. B., G. A. Dale, and A. W. Jackson. 2001. "Youth Coaching

Preferences of Adolescent Athletes and Their Parents." *Journal of Sport Behavior* 24, no. 2: 197–212.

Mautner, K., and J. Blazuk. 2015. "Overuse Throwing Injuries in Skeletally Immature Athletes—Diagnosis, Treatment, and Prevention." *Current Sports Medicine Reports* 14, no. 3: 209–14.

Miller, A. E., J. D. MacDougall, M. A. Tarnopolsky, and D. G. Sale. 1993. "Gender Differences in Strength and Muscle Fiber Characteristics." *European Journal of Applied Physiology and Occupational Physiology* 66, no. 3: 254–62.

Mitchell, I. D., R. Neil, R. Wadey, and S. Hanton. 2007. "Gender Differences in Athletes' Social Support during Injury Rehabilitation." *Journal of Sport and Exercise Psychology* 29, supp. 1 : S189–S190.

Morning Edition. 2016. "To Get a College Scholarship: Forget the Field, Hit the Books." NPR Opinion, November 16. Hosted by David Greene. https://www.npr.org/2016/11/16/502274825/forget-the-fields-hit-the-books-to-get-a-college-scholarship.

National Alliance for Youth Sports. 2013. "Parents' Code of Ethics." National Alliance for Youth Sports. https://www.nays.org/paysonline/members/pdf/Parents-COE.pdf.

National Collegiate Athletic Association. 2019. "Estimated Probability of Competing in College Athletics." Accessed June 22, 2019. https://ncaaorg.s3.amazonaws.com/research/pro_beyond/2019RES_ProbabilityBeyondHSFiguresMethod.pdf.

National Sleep Foundation. 2015. "National Sleep Foundation Recommends New Sleep Times." National Sleep Foundation, February 2. https://www.sleepfoundation.org/press-release/national-sleep-foundation-recommends-new-sleep-times/page/0/1.

Omli, J., and D. M. Wiese-Bjornstal. 2011. "Kids Speak: Preferred Parental Behavior at Youth Sport Events." *Research Quarterly for Exercise and Sport* 82, no. 4: 702–11. doi: 10.1080/02701367.2011.10599807.

Payne, V. G., J. R. Morrow Jr., L. Johnson, and S. N. Dalton. 1997. "Resistance Training in Children and Youth: A Meta-analysis." *Research Quarterly for Exercise and Sport* 68, no. 1: 80–88. doi: 10.1080/02701367.1997.10608869.

Pennington, B. 2005. "Doctors See Big Rise in Injuries for Young Athletes." *New York Times*, February 22.

Piaget, J. 1971. "The Theory of Stages in Cognitive Development." In *Measurement and Piaget*, edited by D. R. Green, M. P. Ford, and G. B. Flamer, 1–11. New York: McGraw-Hill.

Rowland, T. 2005. *Children's Exercise Physiology*. Champaign, Ill.: Human Kinetics.

Sabo, D., and P. Veliz. 2011. *Progress without Equity: The Provision of High School Athletic Opportunity in the United States, by Gender 1993–94 through 2005–06*. East Meadow, N.Y.: Women's Sports Foundation.

Sappenfield, K. 2019. "Parental Influences on Youth Competitive and Recreational Sport: A Battle of Perspectives." Master's thesis, Kinesiology, University of North Carolina at Greensboro.

Seiler, S., J. J. De Koning, and C. Foster. 2007. "The Fall and Rise of the Gender Difference in Elite Anaerobic Performance 1952–2006." *Medicine* and *Science in Sports and Exercise* 39, no. 3: 534–40. doi: 10.1249/01. mss.0000247005.17342.2b.

Shell, A. 2017. "Why Families Stretch Their Budgets for High-Priced Youth Sports." *USA Today*, September 5. https://www.usatoday.com/story/money /2017/09/05/why-families-stretch-their-budgets-high-priced-youth-sports /571945001/.

Smith, K. L., P. L. Weir, K. Till, M. Romann, and S. Cobley. 2018. "Relative Age Effects across and within Female Sport Contexts: A Systematic Review and Meta-analysis." *Sports Medicine* 48, no. 6: 1451–78. doi: 10.1007/ s40279-018-0890-8.

Soriano, D. Z., and E. Kerr. 2019. "4 Myths about Athletic Scholarships." *U.S. News and World Report*, June 5. https://www.usnews.com/education/ best-colleges/paying-for-college/articles/2017-10-04/4-myths-about-athletic -scholarships.

Steiner, I. D. 1966. "Models for Inferring Relationships between Group Size and Potential Group Productivity." *Behavioral Sciences* 11, no. 4: 273–83.

Ullrich-French, S., and A. L. Smith. 2006. "Perceptions of Relationships with Parents and Peers in Youth Sport: Independent and Combined Prediction of Motivational Outcomes." *Psychology of Sport and Exercise* 7, no. 2: 193–214.

Visek, A. J., S. M. Achrati, H. Mannix, K. McDonnell, B. S. Harris, and L. DiPietro. 2015. "The Fun Integration Theory: Toward Sustaining Children and Adolescents Sport Participation." *Journal of Physical Activity and Health* 12, no. 3: 424–33. doi: 10.1123/jpah.2013-0180.

Washington County Soccer Club. 2019. "Mission Statement." BartlesvilleSoccer .org. http://bartlesvillesoccer.org/pages/mission-statement.

Weiss, M. R., and L. Williams. 2004. "The *Why* of Youth Sport Involvement: A Developmental Perspective on Motivational Processes." In *Developmental Sport and Exercise Psychology: A Lifespan Perspective*, edited by M. R. Weiss, 223–68. Morgantown, W.V.: Fitness Information Technology.

Wintergreen Research. 2018. "Global Youth Team, League, and Tournament Sports Market, 2018–2024: A $15.5 Billion Market in the US, the Youth Sports Market Rivals the Size of the $14 Billion NFL." Wintergreen Research. https://www.prnewswire.com/news-releases/global-youth-team-league-and -tournament-sports-market-2018-2024-a-15-5-billion-market-in-the-us-the -youth-sports-market-rivals-the-size-of-the-14-billion-nfl-300707069.html.

Wojtys, E. M. 2013. "Sports Specialization vs. Diversification." *Sports Health* 5, no. 3: 212–13. doi: 10.1177/1941738113484130.

Yu, B., and W. E. Garrett. 2007. "Mechanisms of Non-contact ACL Injuries." *British Journal of Sports Medicine* 41, supp. 1: i47–i51. doi: 10.1136/bjsm.2007 .037192.

INDEX